A LASTING JOY

A
LASTING
JOY

An Anthology Chosen
and Introduced by
C. DAY LEWIS

LONDON
GEORGE ALLEN & UNWIN LTD
RUSKIN HOUSE MUSEUM STREET

First published in 1973

© George Allen & Unwin Ltd 1973

ISBN 0 04 808016 0

Printed in Great Britain
in 12 point Barbou type
by W & J Mackay Limited
Chatham

For Tamasin and Daniel

FOREWORD

The story of our working partnership began twenty-five years ago. It ended with the programmes which were shown on BBC-1 after my husband's death. In other words this anthology was designed not just for speaking aloud, but for television. Furthermore, it was to be the first time that BBC-1 had presented a series entirely devoted to poetry, as distinct from the poems that were incorporated into other arts programmes, and the idea of 'using the latest means of communication to put over the oldest of the arts' particularly appealed to Cecil. The invitation came from Norman Swallow, the head of BBC television arts features. He was taking an enormous risk. We three had had many animated, but often inconclusive discussions as to *how* one could present poetry on television, and even if one could do so at all. Reading to a 'live' public, and for sound radio had always seemed far more satisfactory: the one involving an audience, the other allowing for total concentration on the words (for reader and listener) by its very disembodiment and intimacy.

In August 1971, Norman Swallow commissioned us to choose and read the six programmes contained in this book. It was to be a 'convalescent' exercise for my husband, who had had a major operation early in April 1971, and was virtually unable to work. I was the only one of the three of us involved who knew that he was dying of cancer, and had been given a 'possible year' to live.

From the outset we were agreed that each of the programmes would be built on a single theme. These six themes are introduced in my husband's own particular way in this book. For those readers who never heard him speak, I would say that he was endowed with one of the most spell-binding voices I ever heard: in turn gentle, contemplative, passionate, urbane, witty. The articulation was all purity and clarity until the ravages of the disease, which rendered him permanently parched, caused an occasional slurring of speech, only audible to our professional ears. As a poet and also a trained singer, he had an inborn lyricism, sense of rhythm and capacity for breath control, and therefore phrasing. He never lost the hint of Anglo-Irish pronunciation that was his inheritance. In talking to people and about poetry – as will be apparent in these pages – he was never pompous or pedantic, never solemn when he was serious, never lost his infinite capacity for enthusiasm and joy. Neither did he ever reject the commonplace or the much anthologised poem. Rather did he invest them with the nobility that they deserved, and which was so much a part of his nature. I remember in particular wondering at the strength in his frail frame as he said: 'To strive, to seek, to find, and not to yield.' I don't know how he did it.

When we came to film the programmes in January 1972, it had long been apparent to me that he was far too ill to be transported to the BBC Television Centre. This meant that Norman Swallow arranged to bring a television crew to our own house in Greenwich. The series was filmed in our sitting-room. In spite of the obvious drawbacks of main-road traffic outside, we used the pretext to my husband that the atmosphere of our home would be far more intimate than a studio set. In fact we were enabling him to conserve what strength he had, and he would collapse from total exhaustion between filming sessions. As there were power cuts at the time, the BBC supplied a generator. This is the moment when I would like to express my profound gratitude to Norman Swallow the director, A. A. Englander the cameraman, his assistant David Evans, the sound recordist Doug Mawson, and Arthur McMullen – 'our' crew, as we called them – and the other people who, unknown to us, played a part in the making of the programmes. They knew the circumstances, they had appallingly difficult technical obstacles to overcome – even without power cuts. They transformed by far more than their combined skills a painful situation into an exciting new adventure. We were allowed to invite guest readers for two of the programmes, otherwise we read all the poems ourselves. To our great delight Marius Goring joined us for the programme on 'satire and hatred', and John Gielgud for the last. They brought us life, warmth, and their superb talents with a generosity that I shall never forget.

Cecil's genius as a reader of poetry was so to immerse himself in the other poet that he appeared to be re-creating the poem as he read it: he *became* Hardy, Yeats, Wordsworth, Seferis. This is not to deny that he was a *performer*, but to state that he could achieve what most readers strive for and seldom attain – a total identification with other poets, but with all the technique and musicianship of a trained actor and singer.

This then was our swan-song. We had travelled and spoken all over the British Isles and abroad as partners, we had made hundreds of broadcasts on radio together. But this was our first television programme together and it was also our last. He never lived to see these programmes. Number six, on 'death and immortality', was transmitted the week of his death in May 1972, before the series started later in sequence. I had not – never will have – the courage to see them myself. But he chose the title, and although his voice is gone,

> . . . – not the silence after music,
> But the silence of no more music . . .[1]

a lasting joy remains – the joy of having shared with him all those years of reading aloud. It was only one of our many lasting joys.

JILL BALCON
Greenwich, 1973

[1] C. Day Lewis, 'Elegy for a Woman Unknown', *The Room* (Cape, 1965)

11

Publisher's Note

In transforming *A Lasting Joy* from a television series into a book some changes – such as the substitution of 'book' for 'series' and 'section' for 'programme' – have been inevitable, but we have striven to keep editing to a minimum and to preserve C. Day Lewis's voice and mannerisms unchanged. Nevertheless, the idea of turning *A Lasting Joy* into a book was only put forward after C. Day Lewis's death. Any faults the book may have are therefore ours, the virtues his alone.

CONTENTS

Foreword by Jill Balcon   *page* 9

CHILDHOOD   15

HUMAN HEROISM   31

SATIRE AND HATRED   45

LOVE AND FRIENDSHIP   61

TIMES AND SEASONS   77

DEATH AND IMMORTALITY   93

Acknowledgements   107

Index of poems   109

Each part of this book is devoted to a single theme. Each of these themes obviously has as many variations as there are poets. Of the poems we've chosen, some will be very familiar to you. And others we hope will be very unfamiliar. We want to give you the pleasure of listening to old friends and we also want to give you the quite opposite pleasure of meeting strangers, the pleasures of excitement and of interest in what is quite new. It's quite clear to me that poetry is one of the most durable of the products of the human mind and it is this lasting joy of poetry which we hope to convey....

C. DAY LEWIS

CHILDHOOD

I remember, I remember
　The house where I was born,
The little window where the sun
　Came peeping in at morn;
He never came a wink too soon
　Nor brought too long a day;
But now, I often wish the night
　Had borne my breath away.

I remember, I remember
　The roses, red and white,
The violets, and the lily-cups—
　Those flowers made of light!
The lilacs where the robin built,
　And where my brother set
The laburnum on his birth-day—
　The tree is living yet!

I remember, I remember
　Where I was used to swing,
And thought the air must rush as fresh
　To swallows on the wing;
My spirit flew in feathers then
　That is so heavy now,
And summer pools could hardly cool
　The fever on my brow.

I remember, I remember
　The fir trees dark and high;

I used to think their slender tops
　　Were close against the sky:
It was a childish ignorance,
　　But now 'tis little joy
To know I'm farther off from Heaven
　　Than when I was a boy.

'Past and Present'
by Thomas Hood

❋

*Let's begin at the beginning. At our own beginnings. Birth, and
childhood, and then the boy growing up and taking on all the experi-
ences which enlarge him and which help to create the identity which
grows up into manhood. In the first part of this book, the theme re-
appears in variations. The grown-up looking at a child, thinking
about childhood. Then the grown-up remembers his own childhood;
and, of course, there is the childhood of the world itself. You'll see
what poets have made of all these variations, the wonderful response
they make to this wealth of experience and the response they make to
the simplest, the most commonplace – like being born. But, of course,
no experience is commonplace to a good poet. Here, for example, is
Traherne, the seventeenth-century poet, and – though he's grown up –
his eyes are still open in wonder at the thought of coming into the
world.*

From Dust I rise
And out of Nothing now awake;
These brighter Regions which salute mine Eyes
A Gift from God I take:
The Earth, the Seas, the Light, the lofty Skies,
The Sun and Stars are mine; if these I prize.

A Stranger here
Strange things doth meet, strange Glory see,
Strange Treasures lodg'd in this fair World appear,

Strange all and New to me:
But that they *mine* should be who Nothing was,
That Strangest is of all; yet brought to pass.

from 'The Salutation'
by Thomas Traherne

Traherne felt he awoke out of nothing. Wordsworth, in a passage
from his famous ode on 'Intimations of Immortality', said he came
from God. The Wordsworth passage is more eloquent – it has a
grandeur which the other doesn't – but somehow I prefer the simple,
unvarnished faith in the Traherne extract. And, of course, apart
from that I feel that Wordsworth, in the Intimations ode, does get
a bit muddle-headed here and there. . . .

Our birth is but a sleep and a forgetting:
The Soul that rises with us, our life's Star,
    Hath had elsewhere its setting,
        And cometh from afar:
    Not in entire forgetfulness,
    And not in utter nakedness,
But trailing clouds of glory do we come
        From God, who is our home:

from 'Intimations of Immortality from Recollections of Early
Childhood' by William Wordsworth

Now we move on to the child growing up, to Walt Whitman's poem
'There Was a Child Went Forth'. You will notice how, in the poem,
a simple catalogue can become a song of praise.

There was a child went forth every day,
And the first object he look'd upon, that object he became,

And that object became part of him for the day or a certain part
of the day,
Or for many years or stretching cycles of years.

The early lilacs became part of this child,
And grass and white and red morning-glories, and white and red
clover, and the song of the phoebe-bird,
And the Third-month lambs and the sow's pink-faint litter, and
the mare's foal and the cow's calf,
And the noisy brood of the barnyard or by the mire of the pond-
side,
And the fish suspending themselves so curiously below there,
and the beautiful curious liquid,
And the water-plants with their graceful flat heads, all became
part of him.

The field-sprouts of Fourth-month and Fifth-month became
part of him,
Winter-grain sprouts and those of the light-yellow corn, and
the esculent roots of the garden,
And the apple-trees cover'd with blossoms and the fruit after-
ward, and wood-berries, and the commonest weeds by the
road,
And the old drunkard staggering home from the outhouse of
the tavern whence he had lately risen,
And the schoolmistress that pass'd on her way to the school,
And the friendly boys that pass'd, and the quarrelsome boys,
And the tidy and fresh-cheek'd girls, and the barefoot negro boy
and girl,
And all the changes of city and country wherever he went.

His own parents, he that had father'd him and she that had con-
ceiv'd him in her womb and birth'd him,
They gave this child more of themselves than that,
They gave him afterward every day, they became part of him.

The mother at home quietly placing the dishes on the supper-
table,

The mother with mild words, clean her cap and gown, a whole-
some odour falling off her person and clothes as she walks
by,
The father, strong, self-sufficient, manly, mean, anger'd, un-
just,
The blow, the quick loud word, the tight bargain, the crafty
lure,
The family usages, the language, the company, the furniture,
the yearning and swelling heart,
Affection that will not be gainsay'd, the sense of what is real,
the thought if after all it should prove unreal,
The doubts of day-time and the doubts of night-time, the
curious whether and how,
Whether that which appears so is so, or is it all flashes and
specks?
Men and women crowding fast in the streets, if they are not
flashes and specks what are they?
The streets themselves and the facades of houses, and goods in
the windows,
Vehicles, teams, the heavy-plank'd wharves, the huge crossing
at the ferries,
The village on the highland seen from afar at sunset, the river
between,
Shadows, aureola and mist, the light falling on roofs and gables
of white or brown two miles off,
The schooner near by sleepily dropping down the tide, the
little boat slack-tow'd astern,
The hurrying tumbling waves, quick-broken crests, slapping,
The strata of colour'd clouds, the long bar of maroon-tint away
solitary by itself, the spread of purity it lies motionless in,
The horizon's edge, the flying sea-crow, the fragrance of salt
marsh and shore mud,
These become part of that child who went forth every day, and
who now goes, and will always go forth every day.

'There Was a Child Went Forth'
by Walt Whitman

The opposite side of the picture shows us a poet looking at a young girl and thinking how she will have, sooner or later, to be stripped of her childhood fancies, her childhood self and illusions, like a tree stripped of its leaves in autumn – how she will have to take on the lesson of mortality.

> Margaret, are you grieving
> Over Goldengrove unleaving?
> Leaves, like the things of man, you
> With your fresh thoughts care for, can you?
> Ah! as the heart grows older
> It will come to such sights colder
> By and by, nor spare a sigh
> Though worlds of wanwood leafmeal lie;
> And yet you will weep and know why.
> Now no matter, child, the name:
> Sorrow's springs are the same.
> Nor mouth had, no nor mind, expressed
> What heart heard of, ghost guessed:
> It is the blight man was born for,
> It is Margaret you mourn for.

> *'Spring and Fall'*
> *by Gerard Manley Hopkins*

Sometimes children escape this cooling of the heart, this unleafing of their golden grove, by dying young. That's a terribly difficult theme for a poet to handle without either sentimentality or a kind of theatrical stiff upper lip. The great Chinese poet, Po Chü-i, he flourished in the eighth century, he wrote two poems, 'Golden Bells' and 'Remembering Golden Bells', and he avoided this difficulty. And he avoided it by making the father in the first poem rather sour, rather selfish, so when we come to the end – when we come on to the second poem and his emotion really bursts out, we realise he is sincere about it. These poems are translated by Arthur Waley.

When I was almost forty
I had a daughter whose name was Golden Bells.
Now it is just a year since she was born;
She is learning to sit and cannot yet talk.
Ashamed,—to find that I have not a sage's heart:
I cannot resist vulgar thoughts and feelings.
Henceforward I am tied to things outside myself:
My only reward,—the pleasure I am getting now.
If I am spared the grief of her dying young,
Then I shall have the trouble of getting her married.
My plan for retiring and going back to the hills
Must now be postponed for fifteen years!

> 'Golden Bells' by Po Chü-i
> translated by Arthur Waley

Ruined and ill,—a man of two score;
  Pretty and guileless,—a girl of three.
Not a boy,—but still better than nothing:
To soothe one's feeling,—from time to time a kiss!
There came a day,—they suddenly took her from me;
Her soul's shadow wandered I know not where.
And when I remember how just at the time she died
She lisped strange sounds, beginning to learn to talk,
Then I know that the ties of flesh and blood
Only bind us to a load of grief and sorrow.
At last, by thinking of the time before she was born,
By thought and reason I drove the pain away.
Since my heart forgot her, many days have passed
And three times winter has changed to spring.
This morning, for a little, the old grief came back,
Because, in the road, I met her foster-nurse.

> 'Remembering Golden Bells' by Po Chü-i
> translated by Arthur Waley

Here's a very different kind of poem. It imagines an orphan child. She has a pet bird. She loves it but she can't make it eat. This pet bird is obviously a symbol of her own heart which is starved of affection. This is a part of 'The Orphan's Song' by the Victorian poet Sydney Dobell.

I had a little bird,
I took it from the nest;
I prest it, and blest it,
And nursed it in my breast.

I set it on the ground,
I danced round and round,
And sang about it so cheerly,
With 'Hey my little bird, and ho my little bird,
And oh but I love thee dearly!'

I make a little feast
Of food soft and sweet,
I hold it in my breast,
And coax it to eat;

I pit, and I pat,
I call it this and that,
And sing about it so cheerly,
With 'Hey my little bird, and ho my little bird,
And ho but I love thee dearly!'

I may kiss, I may sing,
But I can't make it feed,
It taketh no heed
Of any pleasant thing.

I scolded, and I socked,
But it minded not a whit,
Its little mouth was locked,
And I could not open it.

Tho' with pit, and with pat,
And with this, and with that,
I sang about it so cheerly,
And 'Hey my little bird, and ho my little bird,
And ho but I love thee dearly.'

But when the day was done,
And the room was at rest,
And I sat all alone,
With my birdie in my breast,

And the light had fled,
And not a sound was heard,
Then my little bird
Lifted up its head,

And the little mouth
Loosed its sullen pride,
And it opened, it opened,
With a yearning strong and wide.

Swifter than I speak
I brought it food once more,
But the poor little beak
Was locked as before.

I sat down again,
And not a creature stirred,
I laid the little bird
Again where it had lain;

And again when nothing stirred,
And not a word I said,
Then my little bird,
Lifted up its head,
And the little beak
Loosed its stubborn pride,
And it opened, it opened,
With a yearning strong and wide.

It lay in my breast,
It uttered no cry,
'Twas famished, 'twas famished,
And I couldn't tell why.

I couldn't tell why,
But I saw that it would die,
For all that I kept dancing round and round,
And singing above it so cheerly,
With 'Hey my little bird, and ho my little bird,
And ho but I love thee dearly!'

from 'The Orphan's Song'
by Sidney Dobell

We will come back to childhood presently. Let's look now for a while at the childhood of the world. So many poets and writers have imagined a Golden Age, a time when Nature did all the work and men just lay about enjoying themselves, and some writers have put this Golden Age into the future and they are the people who create Utopias. Virgil, in his Fourth Eclogue, looked forward to a time when a great new cycle of centuries begins, justice returns to earth, the Golden Age returns. And presently he goes on like this . . . .

Traders will retire from the sea, from the pine-built vessels
They used for commerce: every land will be self-supporting.
The soil will need no harrowing, the vine no pruning-knife;
And the tough ploughman may at last unyoke his oxen.
We shall stop treating wool with artificial dyes,
For the ram himself in his pasture will change his fleece's colour,
Now to charming purple, now to a saffron hue,
And grazing lambs will dress themselves in coats of scarlet.

from 'Fourth Eclogue'
by Virgil

I won't say that Virgil is sending up the Golden Age in those last lines but he's certainly treating it with a very light touch, as D. H. Lawrence is using a very light touch in a poem when he is describing the very beginnings of the world, before mankind ever put in an appearance. The poem is called 'Humming-Bird'.

I can imagine, in some otherworld
Primeval-dumb, far back
In that most awful stillness, that only gasped and hummed,
Humming-birds raced down the avenues.

Before anything had a soul,
While life was a heave of Matter, half inanimate,
This little bit chipped off in brilliance
And went whizzing through the slow, vast, succulent stems.

I believe there were no flowers then,
In the world where the humming-bird flashed ahead of creation.
I believe he pierced the slow vegetable veins with his long beak.

Probably he was big
As mosses, and little lizards, they say, were once big.
Probably he was a jabbing, terrifying monster.

We look at him through the wrong end of the long telescope of
    Time,
Luckily for us.

'Humming-Bird'
by D. H. Lawrence

❋

So we come round again to childhood, to people now grown up remembering their own childhood, or their parents or their childhood home, seeing them all through that golden mist which, if we're lucky, memory throws over the past; and it's not difficult to imagine, how this myth of the Golden Age arose from people recalling what they remember as the simplicity, and the innocence, of their childhood days.

William Cowper, for instance, remembers his mother and the
house where he lived as a child.

Where once we dwelt our name is heard no more,
Children not thine have trod my nurs'ry floor;
And where the gard'ner Robin, day by day,
Drew me to school along the public way,
Delighted with my bauble coach, and wrapt
In scarlet mantle warm, and velvet capt,
'Tis now become a history little known,
That once we call'd the past'ral house our own.
Short-liv'd possession! but the record fair
That mem'ry keeps of all thy kindness there,
Still outlives many a storm that has effac'd
A thousand other themes less deeply trac'd.
Thy nightly visits to my chamber made,
That thou might'st know me safe and warmly laid;
Thy morning bounties ere I left my home,
The biscuit, or confectionary plum;
The fragrant waters on my cheeks bestow'd
By thy own hand, till fresh they shone and glow'd:
All this, and more endearing still than all,
Thy constant flow of love, that knew no fall,
Ne'er roughen'd by those cataracts and breaks,
That humour interpos'd too often makes;
All this still legible in mem'ry's page,
And still to be so, to my latest age,
Adds joy to duty, makes me glad to pay
Such honours to thee as my numbers may;
Perhaps a frail memorial, but sincere,
Not scorn'd in heav'n, though little notic'd here.
Could Time, his flight revers'd, restore the hours
When, playing with thy vesture's tissued flow'rs—
The violet, the pink, and jassamine—
I prick'd them into paper with a pin,
(And thou wast happier than myself the while,

Would'st softly speak, and stroke my head, and smile)
Could those few pleasant hours again appear,
Might one wish bring them, would I wish them here?
I would not trust my heart—the dear delight
Seems so to be desir'd, perhaps I might.—
But no:—what here we call our life is such,
So little to be lov'd, and thou so much,
That I should ill requite thee to constrain
Thy unbound spirit into bonds again.

from 'On Receipt of my Mother's Picture out of Norfolk
by William Cowper

Thomas Hardy imagines himself as a child in the cottage at Upper
Bockhampton in Dorset where he was born, sitting with his parents.
His father is playing the fiddle, his mother sitting by the fire, and
the children . . . the children didn't realise the idyllic nature of the
scene in which they were taking part, and they didn't realise it be-
cause, as Hardy tells us they were looking away.

Here is the ancient floor,
Footworn and hollowed and thin,
Here was the former door
Where the dead feet walked in.

She sat here in her chair,
Smiling into the fire;
He who played stood there,
Bowing it higher and higher.

Childlike, I danced in a dream;
Blessings emblazoned that day;
Everything glowed with a gleam;
Yet we were looking away!

'The Self-Unseeing'
by Thomas Hardy

HUMAN HEROISM

The following passage from Alexander Pope sets the tone for the second section of the book; Mankind in all its doubts and limitations, all its errors and contradictions and its heroisms. We may think of heroic poetry as a thing of the past, something simple, grand, noble, but which it is really impossible to write nowadays, something whose characters emerge bigger than life-size, like characters coming at us out of a mist, out of the mists of antiquity. We have perhaps been conned into this idea a little by our half-baked ideas of modern psychology which tells us that all, everyone, including heroes, has feet of clay, as the rest of us of course have.

Know then thyself, presume not God to scan;
The proper study of Mankind is Man.
Placed on this isthmus of a middle state,
A Being darkly wise, and rudely great:
With too much knowledge for the Sceptic side,
With too much weakness for the Stoic's pride,
He hangs between; in doubt to act or rest;
In doubt to deem himself a God, or Beast;
In doubt his Mind or Body to prefer;
Born but to die and reas'ning but to err;
Alike in ignorance, his reason such,
Whether he thinks too little or too much:
Chaos of Thought and Passion, all confused;
Still by himself abused, or disabused;
Created half to rise, and half to fall;
Great lord of all things, yet a prey to all;
Sole judge of Truth, in endless Error hurled:
The glory, jest, and riddle of the world!

from 'An Essay on Man'
by Alexander Pope

Now, I want to set two poems side by side. The first was written by a clergyman called Charles Wolfe who lived in the south-east bit of Ireland, where I happen to come from myself. He was totally unknown to fame, even in his own day, I think, and there's only one poem of his remembered now, a poem that he wrote on an Irish General, Sir John Moore, who was killed during the Peninsular War at Corunna. This poem was hailed by Byron, who was a very stern judge of that kind of thing, as the greatest ode in the English language.

Not a drum was heard, not a funeral note,
　As his corse to the rampart we hurried;
Not a soldier discharged his farewell shot
　O'er the grave where our hero we buried.

We buried him darkly at dead of night,
　The sods with our bayonets turning,
By the struggling moonbeam's misty light
　And the lanthorn dimly burning.

No useless coffin enclosed his breast,
　Not in sheet or in shroud we wound him;
But he lay like a warrior taking his rest
　With his martial cloak around him.

Few and short were the prayers we said,
　And we spoke not a word of sorrow;
But we steadfastly gazed on the face that was dead,
　And we bitterly thought of the morrow.

We thought, as we hollow'd his narrow bed
　And smooth'd down his lonely pillow,
That the foe and the stranger would tread o'er his head,
　And we far away on the billow!

Lightly they'll talk of the spirit that's gone,
　And o'er his cold ashes upbraid him—
But little he'll reck, if they let him sleep on
　In the grave where a Briton has laid him.

But half of our heavy task was done
   When the clock struck the hour for retiring;
And we heard the distant and random gun
   That the foe was sullenly firing.

Slowly and sadly we laid him down,
   From the field of his fame fresh and gory;
We carved not a line, and we raised not a stone,
   But we left him alone with his glory.

*'The Burial of Sir John Moore after Corunna
by Charles Wolfe*

*That's eloquent all right, isn't it? It's simple, it's sincere and it's
certainly not grandiose. One feels that the sentiment is honest and it's
never inflated. Yet there's also a quite different kind of heroism, the
unconscious kind, when you're doing something not at all like a
soldier in the line in the way of duty with your comrades beside you
to help you on, but some quite ordinary action that's transfigured by
the deep impression it makes on some chance onlooker.*

*During the war, I remember, I found myself in the street during
an air raid and popped down into a shelter, which was far too near
the surface, I may say, and there were a number of grown-ups sitting
there, all trembling slightly, bombs bursting all round. In the shelter
there was a small girl, not with any of the adults, and the small girl
was a girl of extreme beauty, perhaps six or seven or eight years old.
She was nursing a doll and she was nursing a doll in the classic
maternal pose as though she was sheltering this little doll against the
erupting skies and this gave me the theme for a poem I wrote a year
or two later.*

In a shelter one night, when death was taking the air
Outside, I saw her, seated apart—a child
Nursing her doll, to one man's vision enisled
With radiance which might have shamed even death to its lair.

35

Then I thought of our Christmas roses at home—the dark
Lanterns comforting us a winter through
With the same dusky flush, the same bold spark
Of confidence, O sheltering child, as you.

Genius could never paint the maternal pose
More deftly than accident had roughed it there,
Setting amidst our terrors, against the glare
Of unshaded bulb and whitewashed brick, that rose.

Instinct was hers, and an earthquake hour revealed it
In flesh—the meek-laid lashes, the glint in the eye
Defying wrath and reason, the arms that shielded
A plaster doll from an erupting sky.

No argument for living could long sustain
These ills: it needs a faithful eye, to have seen all
Love in the droop of a lash and tell it eternal
By one pure bead of its dew-dissolving chain.

Dear sheltering child, if again misgivings grieve me
That love is only a respite, an opal bloom
Upon our snow-set fields, come back to revive me
Cradling your spark through blizzard; drift and tomb.

'In the Shelter'
by C. Day Lewis

✤

*As I've said, the conventional heroic poetry gave you something
larger than life—it gave you Achilles, Odysseus or Don Juan. But
these heroic figures didn't have to be outsize figures of human virtue;
they testified through their legendary magnetic power to the extra-
ordinary potentiality of human kind for Good or Evil.*

*Dryden, in one of his satires, wrote about the Earl of Shaftesbury
and he made him into a heroic figure certainly, but at the same time he
did full justice to the Earl of Shaftesbury's puny physique, to his
lack of principle, to his traitorous propensities, to his restless ambi-
tion and all that kind of thing; and yet, in spite of this playing down,*

36

as well as satirising of Shaftesbury, the passage in which Shaftes-
bury appears is still heroic satire. Read a bit of it now and you'll see
what I mean.

Of these the false *Achitophel* was first,
A Name to all succeeding Ages curst.
For close Designs and crooked Counsels fit,
Sagacious, Bold, and Turbulent of wit,
Restless, unfixt in Principles and Place,
In Pow'r unpleased, impatient of Disgrace;
A fiery Soul, which working out its way,
Fretted the Pigmy Body to decay:
And o'r informed the Tenement of Clay.
A daring Pilot in extremity;
Pleas'd with the Danger, when the Waves went high
He sought the Storms; but, for a Calm unfit,
Would Steer too nigh the Sands to boast his Wit.
Great Wits are sure to Madness near alli'd
And thin Partitions do their Bounds divide;
Else, why should he, with Wealth and Honour blest,
Refuse his Age the needful hours of Rest?
Punish a Body which he could not please,
Bankrupt of Life, yet Prodigal of Ease?
And all to leave what with his Toil he won
To that unfeather'd two-legged thing, a Son:
Got, while his Soul did huddled Notions trie;
And born a shapeless Lump, like Anarchy.
In Friendship false, implacable in Hate,
Resolv'd to Ruine or to Rule the State;
To Compass this the Triple Bond he broke;
The Pillars of the Publick Safety shook,
And fitted *Israel* for a Foreign Yoke;
Then, seiz'd with Fear, yet still affecting Fame,
Usurp'd a Patriot's All-atoning Name.

from 'Absalom and Achitophel'
by John Dryden

The reverse of that dangerous, impatient, powerful man is the un-publicised, gentle, obscure man who is never thought of as a hero, is never written about until Goldsmith wrote about him in 'The Deserted Village'. This is the Vicar of that famous poem.

Near yonder copse, where once the garden smiled,
And still where many a garden flower grows wild;
There, where a few torn shrubs the place disclose,
The village preacher's modest mansion rose.
A man he was, to all the country dear,
And passing rich with forty pounds a year;
Remote from towns he ran his godly race,
Nor e'er had changed, nor wished to change his place;
Unpractised he to fawn, or seek for power,
By doctrines fashioned to the varying hour;
Far other aims his heart had learned to prize,
More skilled to raise the wretched than to rise.
His house was known to all the vagrant train,
He chid their wanderings, but relieved their pain;
The long remembered beggar was his guest,
Whose beard descending swept his aged breast;
The ruined spendthrift, now no longer proud,
Claimed kindred there, and had his claims allowed;
The broken soldier, kindly bade to stay,
Sate by his fire, and talked the night away;
Wept o'er his wounds, or tales of sorrow done,
Shouldered his crutch, and shewed how fields were won.
Pleased with his guests, the good man learned to glow,
And quite forgot their vices in their woe;
Careless their merits, or their faults to scan,
His pity gave ere charity began.
　　　Thus to relieve the wretched was his pride,
And even his failings leaned to Virtue's side;
But in his duty prompt at every call,
He watched and wept, he prayed and felt, for all.
And, as a bird each fond endearment tries,

To tempt its new fledged offspring to the skies;
He tried each art, reproved each dull delay,
Allured to brighter worlds, and led the way.

from 'The Deserted Village'
by Oliver Goldsmith

✻

I want to go back to the mythical as it's handled in two poems. In the
first poem you'll see what George Seferis makes of it. He is a modern
Greek poet, who only died in 1971. He was the winner of the Nobel
Prize for poetry and he was a friend, as it so happens, of ours. In the
poem, he's meditating on the Argonauts, the men who sailed in the
ship Argo in search of the Golden Fleece and on the way there, and
on the way back particularly, they had innumerable adventures and
experiences.

The second piece is taken, on the other hand, from the oldest piece
of poetry we know, the epic of 'Gilgamesh', which dates from a thou-
sand years before Homeric civilisation. The Seferis poem, which is
translated by Rex Warner, starts off with the Argonauts and con-
tinues with them, but it's really a meditation on the theme of travel.
It tells you a lot about the crew of the Argo, how they became one, as
it were, with the ship or with some part of the ship – with the row-
locks, with the rudder, with the mast – and how they become identi-
fied with this until finally each one of them dies off and because the
ship is a coaster, like all Greek shipping was, he's put ashore, is
buried and his oar is stuck into the earth to mark the spot. And all
this, of course, this endless journey, is really about the endless
journey of humanity.

They were good lads, the comrades. They did not grumble
Because of weariness or because of thirst or because of frost.
They had the manner of trees and the manner of waves
That accept the wind and the rain,
Accept the night and the sun,

And in the midst of change they do not change.
They were good lads. Day after day with downcast eyes
They used to sweat at the oar,
Breathing rhythmically,
And their blood flushed up to an obedient skin.
There was a time when they sang, with downcast eyes,
When we passed the desert island with the Arabian figs,
Towards the setting of the sun, beyond the cape
Of dogs that howl.
If it is to know itself, they used to say,
It is into a soul it must look, they used to say.
And the oars beat on the gold of the sea
In the middle of sunset.
Many the capes we passed, many the islands, the sea
Which brings the other sea, sea-gulls and seals.
There were times when unfortunate women with lamentations
Cried out for their children gone,
And others with wild faces looked for Great-Alexander
And glories sunken in the depths of Asia.
We anchored by shores steeped in nocturnal perfumes
Among the singing of birds, waters that left on the hands
The recollection of a great good fortune.
But there was never an end to the journeys.
Their souls became one with the oars and the rowlocks,
With the severe figurehead at the prow,
With the wake of the rudder,
With the water that fractured the image of their faces.
One after another the comrades died
With downcast eyes. Their oars
Indicate the places where they sleep on the shore.

There is none to remember them, and the word is Justice.

'Mythistorema', Part IV, from 'Argonauts'
by George Seferis
translated by Rex Warner

The new translation of 'Gilgamesh' is by an American scholar, Herbert Mason. Like the Argonauts, it's another version of the great poetic theme of the quest. The two friends, Gilgamesh and Enkidu – Gilgamesh is a great city builder – are approaching the forest whose Lord is the terrifying nature divinity whose name is Humbaba. And their mission is to destroy Humbaba. How amazingly modern this version is, this modern interpretation, when you hear it in the words of Herbert Mason – particularly the last section of the poem, which is the bit given here. It's extraordinarily up to date and the modern feeling comes into it and yet it is still the oldest, most ancient epic in the world.

After three days they reached the edge
Of the forest where Humbaba's watchman stood.
Suddenly it was Gilgamesh who was afraid,
Enkidu who reminded him to be fearless.
The watchman sounded his warning to Humbaba.
The two friends moved slowly toward the forest gate.

When Enkidu touched the gate his hand felt numb,
He could not move his fingers or his wrist,
His face turned pale like someone's witnessing a death,
He tried to ask for help
Whom he had just encouraged to move on,
But he could only stutter and hold out
His paralysed hand.

It will pass, said Gilgamesh.
Would you want to stay behind because of that?
We must go down into the forest together.
Forget your fear of death. I will go before you
And protect you. Enkidu followed close behind
So filled with fear he could not think or speak.
Soon they reached the high cedars.

They stood in awe at the foot

Of the green mountain. Pleasure
Seemed to grow from fear for Gilgamesh.
As when one comes upon a path in woods
Unvisited by men, one is drawn near
The lost and undiscovered in himself;
He was revitalised by danger.
They knew it was the path Humbaba made.
Some called the forest 'Hell', and others 'Paradise';
What difference does it make? said Gilgamesh.
But night was falling quickly
And they had no time to call it names,
Except perhaps 'The Dark',
Before they found a place at the edge of the forest
To serve as shelter for their sleep.

from 'Gilgamesh'
translated by Herbert Mason

W. B. Yeats had a naturally myth-making imagination so let's add to our collection the poem he wrote in memory of the two sisters, Eva Gore-Booth and Con Markiewicz, who were daughters of an Anglo-Irish family. They were both a little larger than life; Eva was a social revolutionary and a minor poet; and Con Markiewicz, an Irish revolutionary who joined the Sinn Fein, fought in the Easter Rising, was imprisoned by the English, was released at the Amnesty, then fought again on the side of de Valera and his Irregulars. She was a very much bigger than life-size figure. As girls they lived in the family house at Lissadell, looking over Sligo Bay, and the name of the house alone gave Yeats one of the most melodious lines in English poetry – the opening line to this poem. You can see how, though he disapproved of what the sisters later became – he didn't like women to be involved in public affairs, in politics, and so on – the passionate intensity of his early memories of them couldn't deny their heroic nature. Even in this poem, written a number of years later . . . .

The light of evening, Lissadell,
Great windows open to the south,
Two girls in silk kimonos, both
Beautiful, one a gazelle.
But a raving autumn shears
Blossom from the summer's wreath;
The older is condemned to death,
Pardoned, drags out lonely years
Conspiring among the ignorant.
I know not what the younger dreams—
Some vague Utopia—and she seems,
When withered old and skeleton-gaunt,
An image of such politics.
Many a time I think to seek
One or the other out and speak
Of that old Georgian mansion, mix
Pictures of the mind, recall
That table and the talk of youth,
Two girls in silk kimonos, both
Beautiful, one a gazelle.
Dear shadows, now you know it all,
All the folly of a fight
With a common wrong or right.
The innocent and the beautiful
Have no enemy but time;
Arise and bid me strike a match
And strike another till time catch;
Should the conflagration climb,
Run till all the sages know.
We the great gazebo built,
They convicted us of guilt;
Bid me strike a match and blow.

'In Memory of Eva Gore-Booth
and Con Markiewicz'
by W. B. Yeats

43

*Let me end this part of the book with another very familar poem,
once again on the poetic theme of the quest, namely the last lines of
Tennyson's 'Ulysses'.*

There lies the port; the vessel puffs her sail:
There gloom the dark broad seas. My mariners,
Souls that have toil'd, and wrought, and thought with me—
That ever with a frolic welcome took
The thunder and the sunshine, and opposed
Free hearts, free foreheads—you and I are old;
Old age hath yet his honour and his toil;
Death closes all: but something ere the end,
Some work of noble note, may yet be done,
Not unbecoming men that strove with Gods,
The lights begin to twinkle from the rocks:
The long day wanes: the slow moon climbs: the deep
Moans round with many voices. Come my friends,
'Tis not too late to seek a newer world.
Push off, and sitting well in order smite
The sounding furrows; for my purpose holds
To sail beyond the sunset, and the baths
Of all the western stars, until I die.
It may be that the gulfs will wash us down:
It may be we shall touch the Happy Isles,
And see the great Achilles, whom we knew.
Tho' much is taken, much abides; and tho'
We are not now that strength which in old days
Moved earth and heaven; that which we are, we are;
One equal temper of heroic hearts,
Made weak by time and fate, but strong in will
To strive, to seek, to find, and not to yield.

*from 'Ulysses'
by Alfred Lord Tennyson*

SATIRE
AND
HATRED

Poets don't spend all their time writing about nature or about love or legendary heroes. They can be very good haters and, having this supreme gift for words, they hate more articulately than anyone else. This third part of the book will show you some of the different forms their dislike of people can take, from the most lethal destruction of their victims to high-spirited fun at their expense; to teasing the absurd fellows and sending them up.

But, first, let's have two poems about imaginary hateful people; a traditional ballad called 'The Brown Girl' – a story-poem, that makes my blood run absolutely cold.

'I am as brown as brown can be,
My eyes as black as a sloe;
I am as brisk as a nightingale,
And as wild as any doe.

'My love has sent me a love-letter,
Not far from yonder town,
That he could not fancy me,
Because I was so brown.

'I sent him his letter back again,
For his love I valu'd not,
Whether that he could fancy me
Or whether he could not.

'He sent me his letter back again,
That he lay sick to death,
That I might then go speedily
To give him up his faith.'

Now you shall hear what love she had
Then for this love-sick man;
She was a whole long summer's day
In a mile a going on.

When she came to her love's bed-side,
Where he lay dangerous sick,
She could not for laughing stand
Upright upon her feet.

She had a white wand all in her hand,
And smooth'd it all on his breast;
'In faith and troth come pardon me,
I hope your soul's at rest.'—

'Prithee,' said he, 'forget, forget,
Prithee forget, forgive;
O grant me yet a little space,
That I may be well and live.'—

'O never will I forget, forgive,
So long as I have breath;
I'll dance above your green, green grave
Where you do lie beneath.

'I'll do as much for my true-love
As other maidens may;
I'll dance and sing on my love's grave
A whole twelvemonth and a day.'

'The Brown Girl',
a traditional ballad

*From that all too simple, highly primitive female, we move on to an
infinitely subtle and suave Italian, an Italian Duke. Having got rid
of one wife, he comes to offer for another young girl, another heiress,
no doubt. He is as elegant and deadly as a snake . . . and here
below is 'My Last Duchess'.*

That's my last Duchess painted on the wall,
Looking as if she were alive. I call
That piece a wonder, now: Frà Pandolf's hands

48

Worked busily a day, and there she stands.
Will't please you sit and look at her? I said
'Frà Pandolf' by design, for never read
Strangers like you that pictured countenance,
The depth and passion of its earnest glance,
But to myself they turned (since none puts by
The curtain I have drawn for you, but I)
And seemed as they would ask me, if they durst,
How such a glance came there; so, not the first
Are you to turn and ask thus. Sir, 'twas not
Her husband's presence only, called that spot
Of joy into the Duchess' cheek: perhaps
Frà Pandolf chanced to say 'Her mantle laps
'Over my lady's wrist too much,' or 'Paint
'Must never hope to reproduce the faint
'Half-flush that dies along her throat:' such stuff
Was courtesy, she thought, and cause enough
For calling up that spot of joy. She had
A heart—how shall I say?—too soon made glad,
Too easily impressed; she liked whate'er
She looked on, and her looks went everywhere.
Sir, 'twas all one! My favour at her breast,
The dropping of the daylight in the West,
The bough of cherries some officious fool
Broke in the orchard for her, the white mule
She rode with round the terrace—all and each
Would draw from her alike the approving speech,
Or blush, at least. She thanked men,—good! but thanked
Somehow—I know not how—as if she ranked
My gift of a nine-hundred-years-old name
With anybody's gift. Who'd stoop to blame
This sort of trifling? Even had you skill
In speech—(which I have not) to make your will
Quite clear to such an one, and say, 'Just this
'Or that in you disgusts me; here you miss,
'Or there exceed the mark'—and if she let

Herself be lessoned so, nor plainly set
Her wits to yours, forsooth, and made excuse,
—E'en then would be some stooping; and I choose
Never to stoop. Oh sir, she smiled, no doubt,
Whene'er I passed her; but who passed without
Much the same smile? This grew; I gave commands;
Then all smiles stopped together. There she stands
As if alive. Will't please you rise? We'll meet
The company below, then. I repeat,
The Count your master's known munificence
Is ample warrant that no just pretence
Of mine for dowry will be disallowed;
Though his fair daughter's self, as I avowed
At starting, is my object. Nay, we'll go
Together down, sir. Notice Neptune, though,
Taming a sea-horse, thought a rarity,
Which Claus of Innsbruck cast in bronze for me!

'My Last Duchess'
by Robert Browning

From those imagined horrors we pass on to two real poetic victims.
We don't somehow think of Tennyson as a satirist but Lord Lytton,
in 'The New Timon', attacked Tennyson for accepting a pension for
writing bad poetry, as Lord Lytton put it, whereupon Tennyson rose
up in wrath and delivered this series of knock-out blows in a poem
called 'The New Timon and the Poets' where he uses a combination
of a kind of tremendously blustering schoolboy humour with the
utter, the most utter adult contempt.

We knew him, out of Shakespeare's art,
    And those fine curses which he spoke;
The old Timon, with his noble heart,
    That, strongly loathing, greatly broke.

So died the Old: here comes the New:
   Regard him: a familiar face:
I *thought* we knew him: What, it's you
   The padded man—that wears the stays—

Who kill'd the girls and thrill'd the boys
   With dandy pathos when you wrote,
A Lion, you, that made a noise,
   And shook a mane *en papillotes*.

And once you tried the Muses too:
   You fail'd, Sir: therefore now you turn,
You fall on those who are to you
   As Captain is to Subaltern.

But men of long enduring hopes,
   And careless what this hour may bring,
Can pardon little would-be Popes
   And Brummels, when they try to sting.

An artist, Sir, should rest in art,
   And waive a little of his claim;
To have the deep poetic heart
   Is more than all poetic fame.

But you, Sir, you are hard to please;
   You never look but half content:
Nor like a gentleman at ease
   With moral breadth of temperament.

And what with spites and what with fears,
   You cannot let a body be:
It's always ringing in your ears,
   'They call this man as good as *me*.'

What profits now to understand
   The merits of a spotless shirt—
A dapper boot—a little hand—
   If half the little soul is dirt?

You talk of tinsel! why we see
   The old mark of rouge upon your cheeks.
You prate of nature! you are he
   That spilt his life about the cliques.

A Timon you! Nay, nay, for shame:
   It looks too arrogant a jest—
The fierce old man—to take *his* name,
   You bandbox. Off, and let him rest.

                    'The New Timon and the Poets'
                    by Alfred Lord Tennyson

❋

Equally blistering is Pope's attack on Lord Harvey. Harvey was at court and in fact he wrote some excellent memoirs about his life there, but he and Pope quarrelled over a lady, and that was quite enough for Pope. Pope calls him 'Sporus' in this passage. . . .

Let *Sporus* tremble—*A.* What? that thing of silk,
Sporus, that mere white curd of Ass's milk?
Satire or sense, alas! can *Sporus* feel?
Who breaks a butterfly upon a wheel?
P. Yet let me flap this bug with gilded wings,
This painted child of dirt, that stinks and stings;
Whose buzz the witty and the fair annoys,
Yet wit ne'er tastes, and beauty ne'er enjoys:
So well-bred spaniels civilly delight
In mumbling of the game they dare not bite.
Eternal smiles his emptiness betray,
As shallow streams run dimpling all the way.
Whether in florid impotence he speaks,
And, as the prompter breathes, the puppet squeaks;
Or at the ear of *Eve*, familiar Toad,
Half froth, half venom, spits himself abroad,

In puns, or politics, or tales, or lies,
Or spite, or smut, or rhymes, or blasphemies.
His wit all see-saw, between *that* and *this*,
Now high, now low, now master up, now miss,
And he himself one vile Antithesis.
Amphibious thing! that acting either part,
The trifling head, or the corrupted heart,
Fop at the toilet, flatt'rer at the board,
Now trips a Lady, and now struts a Lord.
Eve's tempter thus the Rabbins have exprest,
A Cherub's face, a reptile all the rest;
Beauty that shocks you, parts that none will trust;
Wit that can creep, and pride that licks the dust.

from 'Epistle to Dr Arbuthnot'
by Alexander Pope

Let's turn to another kind of – well, I don't know exactly what to call it – not hate – there is something aristocratic, fantastic, rough-tongued, certainly, but high-spirited, about Byron's verse when he's making fun of somebody. We seldom feel that he's in such deadly earnest as Pope was. In 'The Vision of Judgement', for example, Byron gave Southey a thorough going-over. He represents Southey at the day of Judgement as a two-faced man, a time-server, a bad poet, an endless scribbler, a bore, and a figure of fun.

Now the bard, glad to get an audience, which
    By no means often was his case below,
Began to cough, and hawk, and hem, and pitch
    His voice into that awful note of woe
To all unhappy hearers within reach
    Of poets when the tide of rhyme's in flow;
But stuck fast with his first hexameter,
Not one of all whose gouty feet would stir.

But ere the spavin'd dactyls could be spurr'd
    Into recitative, in great dismay
Both Cherubim and seraphim were heard
    To murmur loudly through their long array;
And Michael rose ere he could get a word
    Of all his founder'd verses under way,
And cried, 'For God's sake stop, my friend! 'twere best—
Non Di, non homines—you know the rest.'

Then Michael blew his trump, and still'd the noise
    With one still greater, as is yet the mode
On earth besides; except some grumbling voice.
    Which now and then will make a slight inroad
Upon decorous silence, few will twice
    Lift up their lungs when fairly overcrow'd;
And now the bard could plead his own bad cause,
With all the attitudes of self-applause.

He said—(I only give the heads)—he said,
    He meant no harm in scribbling; 'twas his way
Upon all topics; 'twas, besides, his bread,
    Of which he butter'd both sides; 'twould delay
Too long the assembly (he was pleased to dread),
    And take up rather more time than a day,
To name his works—he would but cite a few—
'Wat Tyler'—'Rhymes on Blenheim'—'Waterloo.'

He had written praises of a regicide;
    He had written praises of all kings whatever;
He had written for republics far and wide,
    And then against them bitterer than ever;
For pantisocracy he once had cried
    Aloud, a scheme less moral than 'twas clever;
Then grew a hearty anti-jacobin—
Had turn'd his coat—and would have turn'd his skin.

He had sung against all battles, and again
   In their high praise and glory; he had call'd
Reviewing 'the ungentle craft,' and then
   Become as base a critic as e'er crawl'd—
Fed, paid, and pamper'd by the very men
   By whom his muse and morals had been maul'd:
He had written much blank verse, and blanker prose,
And more of both than anybody knows.

He had written Wesley's life:—here turning round
   To Satan, 'Sir, I'm ready to write yours,
In two octavo volumes, nicely bound,
   With notes and preface, all that most allures
The pious purchaser; and there's no ground
   For fear, for I can choose my own reviewers:
So let me have the proper documents,
That I may add you to my other saints.'

He ceased, and drew forth an MS; and no
   Persuasion on the part of devils, saints,
Or angels, now could stop the torrent; so
   He read the first three lines of the contents;
But at the fourth, the whole spiritual show
   Had vanish'd, with variety of scents,
Ambrosial and sulphureous, as they sprang,
Like lightning, off from his 'melodious twang'.

Those grand heroics acted as a spell:
   The angels stopp'd their ears and plied their pinions;
The devils ran howling, deafen'd, down to hell;
   The ghosts fled, gibbering, for their own dominions—
(For 'tis not yet decided where they dwell,
   And I leave every man to his opinions);
Michael took refuge in his trump—but, lo!
His teeth were set on edge, he could not blow!

         from 'The Vision of Judgement'
         by Lord Byron

Next died the Widow Goe, an active dame,
Famed ten miles round, and worthy all her fame;
She lost her husband when their loves were young,
But kept her farm, her credit, and her tongue:
Full thirty years she ruled, with matchless skill,
With guiding judgement and resistless will;
Advice she scorn'd, rebellions she suppress'd,
And sons and servants bow'd at her behest.
Like that great man's, who to his Saviour came,
Were the strong words of this commanding dame;—
'Come,' if she said, they came, if 'go,' were gone;
And if 'do this,'—that instant it was done:
Her maidens told she was all eye and ear,
In darkness saw and could at distance hear;—
No parish-business in the place could stir,
Without direction or assent from her;
In turn she took each office as it fell,
Knew all their duties, and discharged them well;
The lazy vagrants in her presence shook,
And pregnant damsels fear'd her stern rebuke;
She look'd on want with judgement clear and cool,
And felt with reason and bestow'd by rule;
She match'd both sons and daughters to her mind,
And lent them eyes, for Love, she heard, was blind;
Yet ceaseless still she throve, alert, alive,
The working bee, in full or empty hive;
Busy and careful, like that working bee,
No time for love nor tender cares had she;

But when our farmers made their amorous vows,
She talk'd of market-steeds and patent ploughs.
Not unemploy'd her evenings pass'd away,
Amusement closed, as business waked the day;
When to her toilet's brief concern she ran,
And conversation with her friends began,
Who all were welcome, what they saw, to share;
And joyous neighbours praised her Christmas fare,
That none around might, in their scorn, complain
Of Gossip Goe as greedy in her gain.
   Thus long she reign'd, admired, if not approved;
Praised, if not honour'd; fear'd, if not beloved;—
When, as the busy days of Spring drew near,
That call'd for all the forecast of the year;
When lively hope the rising crops survey'd,
And April promised what September paid;
When stray'd her lambs where gorse and greenwood grow;
When rose her grass in richer vales below;
When pleased she look'd on all the smiling land,
And viewed the hinds, who wrought at her command;
(Poultry in groups still follow'd where she went;)
Then dread o'ercame her,—that her days were spent.
   'Bless me! I die, and not a warning giv'n,—
With *much* to do on Earth, and ALL for Heav'n!—
No reparation for my soul's affairs,
No leave petition'd for the barn's repairs;
Accounts perplex'd, my interest yet unpaid,
My mind unsettled, and my will unmade;—
A lawyer haste, and in your way, a priest;
And let me die in one good work at least.'
She spake, and, trembling, dropp'd upon her knees,
Heaven in her eye and in her hand her keys;
And still the more she found her life decay,
With greater force she grasp'd those signs of sway:
Then fell and died!—In haste her sons drew near,
And dropp'd, in haste, the tributary tear,

Then from th' adhering clasp the keys unbound,
And consolation for their sorrow found.

from 'The Parish Register'
by George Crabbe

❊

*Last in this span from black hatefulness to bitter hatred comes –
what shall I call it? – The gentle indulgence of sending someone up.
You only find it, I think, in fairly modern poetry. Perhaps we're
getting a bit more tolerant nowadays. Anyway, here, first, is the
Victorian poet Arthur Hugh Clough. He's sending himself up in the
person of the utterly indecisive hero of 'Amours de Voyage', who is
writing from Italy to a friend in England and the hero of this poem is
pursuing very, very faintly a girl called Mary Trevellyn – he can't
make up his mind whether to propose marriage to her or not.*

I am in love, meantime, you think; no doubt you would think so.
I am in love, you say; with those letters, of course, you would
    say so.
I am in love, you declare. I think not so; yet I grant you
It is a pleasure indeed to converse with this girl. Oh, rare gift,
Rare felicity, this! she can talk in a rational way, can
Speak upon subjects that really are matters of mind and of
    thinking,
Yet in perfection retain her simplicity; never, one moment,
Never, however you urge it, however you tempt her, consents
    to
Step from ideas and fancies and loving sensations to those vain
Conscious understandings that vex the minds of mankind.
No, though she talk, it is music; her fingers desert not the keys;
    'tis
Song, though you hear in the song the articulate vocables
    sounded,
Syllabled singly and sweetly the words of melodious meaning.

I am in love, you say: I do not think so, exactly.
Oh, 'tisn't manly, of course, 'tisn't manly, this method of
    wooing;
'Tisn't the way very likely to win. For the woman, they tell you,
Ever prefers the audacious, the wilful, the vehement hero;
She has no heart for the timid, the sensitive soul; and for know-
    ledge,—
Knowledge, O ye Gods!—when did they appreciate know-
    ledge?
Wherefore should they, either? I am sure I do not desire it.
  Ah, and I feel too, Eustace, she cares not a tittle about me!
(Care about me, indeed! and do I really expect it?)
But my manner offends; my ways are wholly repugnant;
Every word that I utter estranges, hurts, and repels her;
Every moment of bliss that I gain, in her exquisite presence,
Slowly, surely, withdraws her, removes her, and severs her
    from me.
Not that I care very much!—any way I escape from the boy's
    own
Folly, to which I am prone, of loving where it is easy.
Not that I mind very much! Why should I? I am not in love,
    and
Am prepared, I think, if not by previous habit,
Yet in the spirit beforehand for this and all that is like it;
It is an easier matter for us contemplative creatures,
Us upon whom the pressure of action is laid so lightly;
We, discontented indeed with things in particular, idle,
Sickly, complaining, by faith, in the vision of things in general,
Manage to hold on our way without, like others around us,
Seizing the nearest arm to comfort, help, and support us.
Yet, after all, my Eustace, I know but little about it.
All I can say for myself, for present alike and for past, is,
Mary Trevellyn, Eustace, is certainly worth your acquaintance.
You couldn't come, I suppose, as far as Florence to see her?

from 'Amours de Voyage'
by Arthur Hugh Clough

The Alexandrian Greek poet, Cavafy, made a corner in the Graeco-Roman Empire. He adored poking fun at minor potentates and we'll end with the poem he calls 'A Sovereign from Western Libya', translated by Rae Dalven.

Aristomenes, son of Menelaus,
a sovereign from Western Libya,
was generally liked in Alexandria
during the ten days he sojourned there.
Like his name, his dress, also, decorously Greek.
He gladly accepted honors, but
he did not seek them; he was modest.
He would buy Greek books,
especially on history and philosophy.
But above all he was a man of few words.
He must be profound in his thoughts, people said,
and for such men it is natural not to talk much.

He was neither profound in his thoughts, nor anything else.
Just an ordinary, ridiculous man.
He took a Greek name, dressed like the Greeks;
learned more or less to behave like the Greeks;
and his soul shuddered with fear lest he chance
to mar a rather favorable impression
by speaking the Greek language with fearful barbarisms,
and the Alexandrians would find him out,
as is their habit, the horrible wretches.

That is why he restricted himself to a few words,
fearfully observing his cases and pronunciation;
and he suffered not a little having
whole conversations piled up inside him.

'A Sovereign from Western Libya'
by C. P. Cavafy
translated by Rae Dalven

LOVE
AND
FRIENDSHIP

Love. Well, we think of love as the richest and most diverse theme of poetry, especially when we include in it friendship, which, of course, we ought to do, as one of love's greatest variations. But when I started thinking about the list of the poems I'd sketched out to include in this section, I was rather appalled to find how many of them – particularly those written by English writers – were unhappy poems. The English don't seem to write much about happy love: about discontented love, about regretted love, about unsatisfied love, about the beloved dead – yes; but when a poet has a happy love on his hands, he seldom seems to want to write about it, to waste his breath on it. You take one of the earliest and finest of English love lyrics, written by the Tudor poet, Thomas Wyatt – 'They flee from me that sometime did me seek'.

They flee from me that sometime did me seek,
    With naked foot stalking in my chamber.
I have seen them gentle, tame and meek,
    That now are wild and do not remember
    That sometime they put themselves in danger
        To take bread at my hand; and now they range
        Busily seeking with a continual change.

Thankt be fortune, it hath been otherwise
    Twenty times better; but once, in special,
In thin array, after a pleasant guise,
    When her loose gown from her shoulders did fall,
    And she me caught in her arms long and small,
        Therewith all sweetly did me kiss,
        And softly said: 'Dear heart how like you this?'

It was no dream; I lay broad waking:
    But all is turned, thorough my gentleness
Into a strange fashion of forsaking;
    And I have leave to go of her goodness,
    And she also to use new-fangleness.

But since that I so kindly am served,
I would fain know what she hath deserved.

'They Flee from Me'
by Sir Thomas Wyatt

✳

*Wyatt had his hour, he had his unforgettable experience. Emily
Brontë never had a living lover to commemorate. Many of her
apparently most passionate love poems were part of a thing called
the Gondal Saga, written in prose and verse – Emily wrote most of
her poems in it. It was based partly on Walter Scott, partly on
Byron. Most of this tremendously Gothic production she wrote in
company with her sister, Anne, but this particular poem, perhaps her
most famous one, 'Cold in the earth', must certainly have been in
memory of her dead brother, Branwell, with whom she had a parti-
cularly close family bond. It is one of the most marvellous and
passionate poems, in quite a different way from the Wyatt, that you
can hope to find in the English language.*

Cold in the earth, and the deep snow piled above thee!
Far, far removed, cold in the dreary grave!
Have I forgot, my Only Love, to love thee,
Severed at last by Time's all-wearing wave? . . .

Cold in the earth, and fifteen wild Decembers
From those brown hills have melted into spring—
Faithful, indeed, is the spirit that remembers
After such years of change and suffering!

Sweet Love of youth, forgive if I forget thee
While the World's tide is bearing me along:
Sterner desires and darker hopes beset me,
Hopes which obscure, but cannot do thee wrong.

No other sun has lightened up my heaven;
No other star has ever shone for me:

All my life's bliss from thy dear life was given—
All my life's bliss is in the grave with thee.

But, when the days of golden dreams had perished
And even Despair was powerless to destroy,
Then did I learn how existence could be cherished,
Strengthened and fed without the aid of joy;

Then did I check the tears of useless passion,
Weaned my young soul from yearning after thine;
Sternly denied its burning wish to hasten
Down to that tomb already more than mine!

And even yet, I dare not let it languish,
Dare not indulge in Memory's rapturous pain;
Once drinking deep of that divinest anguish,
How could I seek the empty world again?

> 'R. Alcona to J. Brenzaida' (Remembrance)
> by Emily Brontë

*Those last two poems – you can say they're straightforward, they give
you moods, they give you states of mind, which are not open to ques-
tion – you don't want to argue about them. But in the next poem you
get a lyric simplicity, certainly, but this is complicated towards the
end of the poem by subtlety, by argument. The poet writes at first as
though he should be quite happy with his beloved, that initially
everything seems to be going well with them; but, no, he can't help
feeling dissatisfied because – why? – because there's not a perfect
unity between him and his wife.*

> I wonder do you feel to-day
>   As I have felt since, hand in hand,
> We sat down on the grass, to stray
>   In spirit better through the land,
> This morn of Rome and May?

65

For me, I touched a thought, I know,
  Has tantalised me many times,
(Like turns of thread the spiders throw
  Mocking across our path) for rhymes
To catch at and let go.

Help me to hold it! First it left
  The yellowing fennel, run to seed
There, branching from the brickwork's cleft,
  Some old tomb's ruin: yonder weed
Took up the floating weft,

Where one small orange cup amassed
  Five beetles,—blind and green they grope
Among the honey-meal: and last,
  Everywhere on the grassy slope
I traced it. Hold it fast!

The champaign with its endless fleece
  Of feathery grasses everywhere!
Silence and passion, joy and peace,
  An everlasting wash of air—
Rome's ghost since her decease.

Such life here, through such lengths of hours,
  Such miracles performed in play,
Such primal naked forms of flowers,
  Such letting nature have her way
While heaven looks from its towers!

How say you? Let us, O my dove,
  Let us be unashamed of soul,
As earth lies bare to heaven above!
  How is it under our control
To love or not to love?

I would that you were all to me,
  You that are just so much, no more.
Nor yours nor mine, nor slave nor free!

Where does the fault lie? What the core
O' the wound, since wound must be?

I would I could adopt your will,
   See with your eyes, and set my heart
Beating by yours, and drink my fill
   At your soul's springs,—your part my part
In life, for good and ill.

No. I yearn upward, touch you close,
   Then stand away. I kiss your cheek,
Catch your soul's warmth,—I pluck the rose
   And love it more than tongue can speak—
Then the good minute goes.

Already how am I so far
   Out of that minute? Must I go
Still like the thistle-ball, no bar,
   Onward, whenever light winds blow,
Fixed by no friendly star?

Just when I seemed about to learn!
   Where is the thread now? Off again!
The old trick! Only I discern—
   Infinite passion, and the pain
Of finite hearts that yearn.

'Two in the Campagna'
by Robert Browning

I think women, on the whole, are too sensible to get unduly worried at being unable to merge heart and soul into the souls of their husbands or lovers. They probably find more useful the kind of practical advice given to them by the poet Praed in these stanzas to Araminta. Praed, of course, is speaking in the personality of a girl-friend of Araminta who was giving her serious advice about the people she should not, at any cost, accept.

You tell me you're promised a lover,
　My own Araminta, next week;
Why cannot my fancy discover
　The hue of his coat and his cheek?
Alas! If he look like another,
　A vicar, a banker, a beau,
Be deaf to your father and mother,
　My own Araminta, say 'No!'

If he wears a top-boot in his wooing,
　If he comes to you riding a cob,
If he talks of his baking or brewing,
　If he puts up his feet on the hob,
If he ever drinks port after dinner,
　If his brow or his breeding is low,
If he calls himself 'Thompson' or 'Skinner',
　My own Araminta, say 'No!'

If he studies the news in the papers
　While you are preparing the tea,
If he talks of the damps or the vapours
　While moonlight lies soft on the sea,
If he's sleepy while you are capricious,
　If he has not a musical 'Oh!'
If he does not call Werther delicious,—
　My own Araminta, say 'No!'

If he ever sets foot in the City
　Among the stockbrokers and Jews,
If he has not a heart full of pity,
　If he don't stand six feet in his shoes,
If his lips are not redder than roses,
　If his hands are not whiter than snow,
If he has not the model of noses,—
　My own Araminta, say 'No!'

If he speaks of a tax or a duty,
　If he does not look grand on his knees,

If he's blind to a landscape of beauty,
  Hills, valleys, rocks, waters, and trees,
If he dotes not on desolate towers,
  If he likes not to hear the blast blow,
If he knows not the language of flowers,—
  My own Araminta, say 'No!'

He must walk—like a god of old story
  Come down from the home of his rest;
He must smile—like the sun in his glory
  On the buds he loves ever the best;
And oh! from its ivory portal
  Like music his soft speech must flow!—
If he speak, smile, or walk like a mortal,
  My own Araminta, say 'No!'

Don't listen to tales of his bounty,
  Don't hear what they say of his birth,
Don't look at his seat in the county,
  Don't calculate what he is worth;
But give him a theme to write verse on,
  And see if he turns out his toe;
If he's only an excellent person,—
  My own Araminta, say 'No!'

from 'A Letter of Advice'
by W. M. Praed

❋

*Let's cast a quick look now at friendship. There are so many reasons
why one makes friends: compatability of temperament, difference of
temperament, chance association, advantage, even, of some kind. I
myself wrote about one of my oldest friends, and here's a stanza of
the poem. We get yet another definition of friendship in this.*

Friendship, I'd guess, has not much more to do
With like minds, shared needs, than with rent or profit:
Nor is it the love which burns to be absolute, then dies
By inches of ill-stitched wounds, of compromise:
But a kind of grace—take it or leave it.
'Keeping up' a friendship means it is through.

> *from 'For Rex Warner on His Sixtieth Birthday'*
> *by C. Day Lewis*

But I don't know a poem where the warmth of friendship is felt so
bluffly, so unequivocably, as in the old ballad by Charles Dibdin
about Tom Bowling. You feel this is really what his shipmates felt
about Tom and what they thought about him and, of course, what
they hoped for him; and I'm going to follow this with a poem by Po
Chü-i. The Chinese are the great masters of poetry about friendship,
as gentle and dreamlike as Tom Bowling is bluff and forthright. But
these poems, written so far afield, are linked by one thing, they're
both about dead friends.

Here, a sheer hulk, lies poor Tom Bowling,
The darling of our crew;
No more he'll hear the tempest howling,
For death has broached him to.
His form was of the manliest beauty,
His heart was kind and soft;
Faithful below Tom did his duty,
And now he's gone aloft.

Tom never from his word departed,
His virtues were so rare;
His friends were many, and true hearted,
His Poll was kind and fair.
And then he'd sing so blithe and jolly,

Ah! many's the time and oft;
But mirth is turned to melancholy,
For Tom is gone aloft.

Yet shall poor Tom find pleasant weather,
When He, Who all commands,
Shall give, to call life's crew together,
The word to pipe all hands.
Thus Death, who kings and tars dispatches,
In vain Tom's life has doffed;
For though his body's under hatches,
His soul is gone aloft.

'Tom Bowling'
by Charles Dibdin

At night I dreamt I was back in Ch'ang-an;
I saw again the faces of old friends.
And in my dreams, under an April sky,
They led me by the hand to wander in the spring winds.
Together we came to the ward of Peace and Quiet;
We stopped our horses at the gate of Yüan Chên.
Yüan Chên was sitting all alone;
When he saw me coming, a smile came to his face.
He pointed back at the flowers in the western court;
Then opened wine in the northern summer-house.
He seemed to be regretting that joy will not stay;
That our souls had met only for a little while,
To part again with hardly time for greeting.
I woke up and thought him still at my side;
I put out my hand; there was nothing there at all.

'Dreaming that I Went with Li and Yü to Visit Yüan Chên'
by Po Chü-i
translated by Arthur Waley

So back we come to love. To love remembered and regretted; the poet's most fruitful theme. But one aspect of love poetry I seem to have forgotten and that is the piece of outrageous flattery, of wonderful exaggeration, which vied for centuries with the 'gather ye roses while ye may' theme. One of the cavalier poets of the seventeenth century, Thomas Carew, wrote, I think, a peculiarly excellent lyric poem in this vein; it's strengthened by certain light allusions, philosophical allusions and scientific allusions, which give it strength, a little strength and ballast, so to speak, and its seriousness carries it beyond the usual flim-flam of mere gallant flattery.

Ask me no more where Jove bestows,
When June is past, the fading rose;
For in your beauty's orient deep
These flowers, as in their causes, sleep.

Ask me no more whither do stray
The golden atoms of the day;
For in pure love heaven did prepare
Those powders to enrich your hair.

Ask me no more whither doth haste
The nightingale when May is past;
For in your sweet dividing throat
She winters and keeps warm her note.

Ask me no more where those stars 'light
That downwards fall in dead of night;
For in your eyes they sit, and there
Fixed, become as in their sphere.

Ask me no more if east or west
The Phoenix builds her spicy nest;
For unto you at last she flies,
And in your fragrant bosom dies.

Thomas Carew

Let me end with three bits of poetry, each by a quite different kind of writer, each written in a totally different way from the other two. But they have in common the poignancy of an older man looking back to a love affair of his youth, meditating upon it, giving us the purest essence of the love which, through a lifetime, he's distilled from it; and so accepting the experience he has passed through that we can all listen to his words and become exalted again and reconciled with our own memories of our own loves of our lives.

First, two similes produced by George Seferis in his poem The 'Thrush', translated by Rex Warner.

It is like
At the end of your youth you happen to be in love
With a woman who has kept her beauty. Holding
Her naked body in the noon, always
You fear the memory that surges up
To your embrace, you fear the kiss betraying you
To other beds which now are in time past,
And yet, for all that, there are ghosts might stalk there
Easily, so easily, and bring to life
Images to the mirror, bodies that were once,
And all the lusts they had then.

It is like
Coming back from a foreign land you chance to open
An old chest that for long has been locked up;
And there you find bits and pieces of the dresses
You wore in lovely times, in lighted revels
Of many colours, mirrored, which all fade,
And remains only the perfume of the absence
Of a young face.

from The 'Thrush'
by George Seferis
translated by Rex Warner

I find those lines utterly magical. And no less magical is this little poem called 'The Afternoon Sun' by Constantine Cavafy. He was an Alexandrian Greek poet who lives on into this century. And in this poem he's simply revisiting a room where he and his lover used to meet. But the poem is absolutely steeped in the deepest human loss and poetic feeling.

This room, how well I know it.
Now they are rented this one and the next
As business offices. The whole house has become
Offices for agents, and merchants, and Companies.

O how familiar it is, this room.

Near the door just here there was the sofa,
And in front of it a Turkish carpet;
Close by the shelf with two yellow vases.
On the right; no, opposite, a wardrobe with a mirror.
In the middle a table where he used to write;
And the three big wicker chairs.
At the side of the window was the bed
Where we made love so many times.

They must still be somewhere the poor old things.

At the side of the window was the bed;
The afternoon sun fell on it half-way up.

. . . One afternoon at four o'clock, we parted
Only for a week. . . . Alas,
That week became perpetual.

'The Afternoon Sun'
by C. P. Cavafy
translated by John Mavrogordato

And last, Thomas Hardy's great farewell to love, one of the poems written after his first wife had died, and when the poet himself was seventy or more years of age.

As I drive to the junction of lane and highway,
　And the drizzle bedrenches the waggonette,
I look behind at the fading byway,
　And see on its slope, now glistening wet,
　　　Distinctly yet

Myself and a girlish form benighted
　In dry March weather. We climb the road
Beside a chaise. We had just alighted
　To ease the sturdy pony's load
　　　When he sighed and slowed.

What we did as we climbed, and what we talked of
　Matters not much, nor to what it led,—
Something that life will not be balked of
　Without rude reason till hope is dead,
　　　And feeling fled.

It filled but a minute. But was there ever
　A time of such quality, since or before,
In that hill's story? To one mind never,
　Though it has been climbed, foot-swift, foot-sore,
　　　By thousands more.

Primaeval rocks form the road's steep border,
　And much have they faced there, first and last,
Of the transitory in Earth's long order;
　But what they record in colour and cast
　　　Is—that we two passed.

And to me, though Time's unflinching rigour,
    In mindless rote, has ruled from sight
The substance now, one phantom figure
    Remains on the slope, as when that night
        Saw us alight.

I look and see it there, shrinking, shrinking,
    I look back at it amid the rain
For the very last time; for my sand is sinking,
    And I shall traverse old love's domain
        Never again.

'At Castle Boterel'
by Thomas Hardy

TIMES
AND
SEASONS

I wasn't quite sure what to call this section. Most of the poems are about nature; but even in cities we are brushed by nature, so let's call it 'Times and Seasons'. It's important at the start to realise how subjective is one's response to nature. As Coleridge said in his great Dejection Ode, 'We receive but what we give'. Here is a passage from this wonderfully true and sad poem. It's taken from the first edition of Sibylline Leaves, *which was published in 1817 and in which this famous Dejection Ode first appeared.*

A grief without a pang, void, dark and drear,
   A stifled, drowsy, unimpassion'd grief,
   Which finds no natural outlet, no relief,
      In word, or sigh, or tear—
O Lady! in this wan and heartless mood,
To other thoughts by yonder throstle woo'd,
   All this long eve, so balmy and serene,
Have I been gazing on the western sky,
   And its peculiar tint of yellow green:
And still I gaze—and with how blank an eye!
And those thin clouds above, in flakes and bars,
That give away their motion to the stars;
Those stars, that glide behind them or between,
Now sparkling, now bedimm'd, but always seen;
Yon crescent Moon, as fix'd as if it grew
In its own cloudless, starless lake of blue;
I see them all so excellently fair,
I see, not feel how beautiful they are!

      My genial spirits fail,
      And what can these avail,
To lift the smoth'ring weight from off my breast?
      It were a vain endeavor,
      Though I should gaze for ever
On that green light that lingers in the west:

79

I may not hope from outward forms to win
The passion and the life, whose fountains are within.

O Lady! we receive but what we give,
And in our life alone does nature live:
Ours is her wedding-garment, ours her shroud!
  And would we aught behold, of higher worth,
Than that inanimate cold world allow'd
To the poor loveless ever-anxious crowd,
  Ah! from the soul itself must issue forth,
A light, a glory, a fair luminous cloud
      Enveloping the Earth—
And from the soul itself must there be sent
  A sweet and potent voice, of its own birth,
Of all sweet sounds the life and element!

from 'Dejection: an Ode'
by Samuel Taylor Coleridge

❋

Wordsworth, in his famous Intimations Ode, has one or two lines
that remind one of that Dejection Ode of Coleridge. 'The things
which I have seen, I now can see no more. But yet I know where'ere I
go there passed away a glory from the earth.' But there is about the
Coleridge poem, and particularly about that simple line 'I see, not
feel, how beautiful they are', a tremendous depth of poignancy which
I don't think Wordsworth ever achieved in the Intimations Ode.
Now, when Wordsworth visited – or, rather, revisited Tintern
Abbey, he wrote immediately afterwards one of his most famous
poems. The passage which follows explores two ways of responding
to nature; the excited, half-animal, ecstatic way of his own boy-
hood, his own young days, and the deeper, more sober, more contem-
plative feeling which nature gives him now, as he is writing the
poem.

And now, with gleams of half-extinguished thought
With many recognitions dim and faint,
And somewhat of a sad perplexity,
The picture of the mind revives again:
While here I stand, not only with the sense
Of present pleasure, but with pleasing thoughts
That in this moment there is life and food
For future years. And so I dare to hope,
Though changed, no doubt, from what I was when first
I came among these hills; when like a roe
I bounded o'er the mountains, by the sides
Of the deep rivers, and the lonely streams,
Wherever nature led: more like a man
Flying from something that he dreads, than one
Who sought the thing he loved. For nature then
(The coarser pleasures of my boyish days,
And their glad animal movements all gone by)
To me was all in all.—I cannot paint
What then I was. The sounding cataract
Haunted me like a passion: the tall rock,
The mountain, and the deep and gloomy wood,
Their colours and their forms, were then to me
An appetite; a feeling and a love,
That had no need of a remoter charm,
By thought supplied, nor any interest
Unborrowed from the eye.—That time is past
And all its aching joys are now no more,
And all its dizzy raptures. Not for this
Faint I, nor mourn nor murmur; other gifts
Have followed; for such loss, I would believe,
Abundant recompense. For I have learned
To look on nature, not as in the hour
Of thoughtless youth; but hearing oftentimes
The still, sad music of humanity,
Nor harsh nor grating, though of ample power
To chasten and subdue. And I have felt

A presence that disturbs me with the joy
Of elevated thoughts; a sense sublime
Of something far more deeply interfused,
Whose dwelling is the light of setting suns,
And the round ocean and the living air,
And the blue sky, and in the mind of man;
A motion and a spirit, that impels
All thinking things, all objects of all thought,
And rolls through all things. Therefore am I still
A lover of the meadows and the woods,
And mountains; and of all that we behold
From this green earth; of all the mighty world
Of eye and ear,—both what they half create,
And what perceive; well pleased to recognise
In nature and the language of the sense
The anchor of my purest thoughts, the nurse,
The guide, the guardian of my heart, and soul
Of all my moral being.

*from 'Lines Composed a Few Miles above Tintern Abbey'
by William Wordsworth*

❋

*Nothing that William Blake wrote can startle us or even shock us
today as it certainly did sometimes startle and shock the Victorians.
But the prophetic poems can still baffle us. So it's nice to get the
occasional lyrical outburst amongst these poems, like the bit about
the voice of spring and the voice of the birds; and we'll follow this
passage at once with a passage about winter from James Thomson's*
The Seasons. *One does tend to think of eighteenth-century nature
verse as loaded with abstractions, cluttered up with idle epithets, but
both extracts are, I think, remarkably vivid and to the point—and
they're both also very spare and sparkling.*

Thou hearest the Nightingale begin the Song of Spring.
The Lark sitting upon his earthy bed, just as the morn
Appears, listen silent; then springing from the wavering Corn-
field, loud
He leads the Choir of Day: trill, trill, trill, trill,
Mounting upon the wings of light into the Great Expanse,
Re-echoing against the lovely blue and shining heavenly Shell,
His little throat labours with inspiration; every feather
On throat and breast and wings vibrates with the effluence
Divine.
All Nature listens silent to him and the awful Sun
Stands still upon the Mountain looking on this little Bird
With eyes of soft humility and wonder, love and awe,
Then loud from their green covert all the Birds begin their Song:
The Thrush, the Linnet and the Goldfinch, Robin and the Wren
Awake the Sun from his sweet reverie upon the Mountain.
The Nightingale again assays his song and thro' the day
And thro' the night warbles luxuriant, every Bird of Song
Attending his loud harmony with admiration and love.

from 'Milton'
by William Blake

With the fierce rage of Winter deep suffus'd,
An icy gale, oft shifting, o'er the pool
Breathes a blue film, and in its mid career
Arrests the bickering stream. The loosened ice,
Let down the flood, and half dissolv'd by day,
Rustles no more; but to the sedgy bank
Fast grows, or gathers round the pointed stone,
A crystal pavement, by the breath of heaven
Cemented firm; till, seiz'd from shore to shore,
The whole imprison'd river growls below.
Loud rings the frozen earth, and hard reflects
A double noise; while, at his evening watch,

The village dog deters the nightly thief;
The heifer lows; the distant waterfall
Swells in the breeze; and, with the hasty tread
Of traveller, the hollow-sounding plain
Shakes from afar. The full ethereal round,
Infinite worlds disclosing to the view,
Shines out intensely keen; and, all one cope
Of starry glitter glows from pole to pole.
    From pole to pole the rigid influence falls,
Through the still night, incessant, heavy, strong,
And seizes Nature fast. It freezes on;
Till morn, late-rising o'er the drooping world,
Lifts her pale eye unjoyous. Then appears
The various labour of the silent night:
Prone from the dripping cave, and dumb cascade,
Whose idle torrents only seem to roar,
The pendant icicle; the frost-work fair,
Where transient hues and fancy'd figures rise;
Wide-spouted o'er the hill the frozen brook,
A livid tract, cold-gleaming on the morn;
The forest bent beneath the plumy wave;
And by the frost refin'd the whiter snow,
Incrusted hard, and sounding to the tread
Of early shepherd, as he pensive seeks
His pining flock, or from the mountain top,
Pleas'd with the slippery surface, swift descends.

from 'Winter'
by James Thomson

*Still in the eighteenth century, let's move from country to town. John
Gay, who wrote 'The Beggar's Opera', also put together a more
solemn or formal poem in the fashionable heroic couplet, a poem he
called 'Trivia'; it's all about London and we can see that two
hundred and fifty years ago people were complaining, just as they are*

complaining now, complaining about the weather, the mud, the
traffic problem and complaining about the appalling difficulties of
crossing the road.

Where the fair columns of St Clement stand,
Whose straiten'd bounds encroach upon the Strand;
Where the low penthouse bows the walker's head,
And the rough pavement wounds the yielding tread;
Where not a post protects the narrow space;
And strung in twines, combs dangle in thy face;
Summon at once thy courage, rouse thy care,
Stand firm, look back, be resolute, beware.
Forth issuing from steep lanes, the collier's steeds
Drag the black load; another cart succeeds,
Team follows team, crowds heap'd on crowds appear,
And wait impatient, 'till the road grow clear.
Now all the pavement sounds with trampling feet,
And the mixt hurry barricades the street,
Entangled here, the waggon's lengthen'd team
Cracks the tough harness: here a pond'rous beam
Lies overturn'd athwart; for slaughter fed
Here lowing bullocks raise their horned head.
Now oaths grow loud, with coaches coaches jar,
And the smart blow provokes the sturdy war;
From the high box they whirl the thong around,
And with the twining lash their shins resound:
Their rage ferments, more dang'rous wounds they try,
And the blood gushes down their painful eye,
And now on foot the frowning warriors light,
And with their pond'rous fists renew the fight;
Blow answers blow, their cheeks are smear'd with blood,
'Till down they fall, and grappling roll in mud.

If wheels bar up the road where streets are crost,
With gentle words the coachman's ear accost:
He ne'er the threat, or harsh command obeys,
But with contempt the spatter'd shoe surveys.

Now man with utmost fortitude thy soul,
To cross the way where carts and coaches roll;
Stay till afar the distant wheel you hear,
Like dying thunder in the breaking air;
Thy foot will slide upon the miry stone,
And passing coaches crush thy tortured bone,
Of wheels enclose the road; on either hand
Pent round with perils, in the midst you stand.
And call for aid in vain; the coachman swears,
And carmen drive, unmindful of thy prayers.
Where wilt thou turn? ah! whither wilt thou fly?
On ev'ry side the pressing spokes are nigh.

from 'Trivia'
by John Gay

✻

Many attempts were made from Dr Johnson and Wordsworth on-
wards to recent times to depict city life in verse and one of the
strangest of them was written a hundred years ago – James Thomson's
'The City of Dreadful Night'. This James Thomson was nothing at
all to do with the eighteenth-century Nature poet you've heard a little
of already. This James Thomson was a desperate pessimist, he was
an atheist, he was a sad sack altogether, but he had a certain share of
integrity and of eloquence and here he's writing this bit of the poem
not so much about London as about all city life.

The mighty river flowing dark and deep,
    With ebb and flood from the remote sea-tides
Vague-sounding through the City's sleepless sleep,
    Is named the River of the Suicides;
For night by night some lorn wretch overweary,
And shuddering from the future yet more dreary,
    Within its cold secure oblivion hides.

One plunges from a bridge's parapet,
    As by some blind and sudden frenzy hurled;
Another wades in slow with purpose set
    Until the waters are above him furled;
Another in a boat with dreamlike motion
Glides drifting down into the desert ocean,
    To starve or sink from out the desert world.

They perish from their suffering surely thus,
    For none beholding them attempts to save,
The while each thinks how soon, solicitous,
    He may seek refuge in the self-same wave;
Some hour when tired of ever-vain endurance
Impatience will forerun the sweet assurance
    Of perfect peace eventual in the grave.

When this poor tragic-farce has palled us long,
    Why actors and spectators doe we stay?—
To fill our so-short *roles* out right or wrong;
    To see what shifts are yet in the dull play
For our illusion; to refrain from grieving
Dear foolish friends by our untimely leaving:
    But those asleep at home, how blest are they!

Yet it is but for one night after all:
    What matters one brief night of dreary pain?
When after it the weary eyelids fall
    Upon the weary eyes and wasted brain;
And all sad scenes and thoughts and feelings vanish
In that sweet sleep no power can ever banish,
    That one best sleep which never wakes again.

from 'The City of Dreadful Night'
by James Thomson

After that painful cry of a disordered mind we come, with some relief, to the calm, the orderliness, the elegance of one of the great eighteenth-century nature poems, William Collins's 'Ode to Evening'. We mustn't forget, though, that William Collins's mind too became disordered towards the end of his life.

If aught of oaten stop, or pastoral song,
May hope, chaste *Eve*, to soothe thy modest ear,
    Like thy own solemn springs,
    Thy springs, and dying gales,

O *Nymph* reserv'd, while now the bright-hair'd sun
Sits on yon western tent, whose cloudy skirts,
    With brede ethereal wove,
    O'erhang his wavy bed:

Now air is hush'd, save where the weak-ey'd bat,
With short shrill shriek flits by on leathern wing,
    Or where the Beetle winds
    His small but sullen horn,

As oft he rises 'midst the twilight path,
Against the pilgrim born in heedless hum:
    Now teach me, Maid compos'd,
    To breathe some soften'd strain,

Whose numbers stealing through thy darkning vale,
May not unseemly with its stillness suit,
    As musing slow, I hail
    Thy genial lov'd return!

For when thy folding star arising shews
His paly circlet, at his warning lamp
    Thy fragrant Hours, and Elves
    Who slept in buds the day,

And many a Nymph who wreaths her brows with sedge,
And sheds the fresh'ning dew, and lovelier still,
    The *Pensive Pleasures* sweet,
    Prepare thy shadowy car.

Then lead, calm Vot'ress, where some sheety lake
Cheers the lone heath, or some time-hallow'd pile,
 Or upland fallows grey
 Reflect its last cool gleam.

Or if chill blust'ring winds, or driving rain,
Prevent my willing feet, be mine the hut,
 That from the mountain's side,
 Views wilds, and swelling floods,

And hamlets brown, and dim-discover'd spires,
And hears their simple bell, and marks o'er all
 Thy dewy fingers draw
 The gradual dusky veil.

While Spring shall pour his show'rs, as oft he wont,
And bathe thy breathing tresses, meekest Eve!
 While Summer loves to sport
 Beneath thy ling'ring light;

While sallow Autumn fills thy lap with leaves;
Or Winter yelling thro' the troublous air,
 Affrights thy shrinking train,
 And rudely rends thy robes;

So long, sure-found beneath the Sylvan shed,
Shall *Fancy, Friendship, Science,* rose-lipp'd *Health,*
 Thy gentlest influence own,
 And hymn thy fav'rite name!

'*Ode to Evening*'
by William Collins

I find the same tranquillity, the same perfect finish, in this little poem by Philip Larkin. Here is a contemporary poet giving the lie to such ignorant nonsense.

> Cut grass lies frail;
> Brief is the breath
> Mown stalks exhale,
> Long, long the death
>
> It dies in the white hours
> Of young-leafed June
> With chestnut flowers,
> With hedges snowlike strewn,
>
> White lilac bowed,
> Lost lanes of Queen Anne's lace,
> And that high-builded cloud
> Moving at summer's pace.
>
> *'Cut Grass'*
> *by Philip Larkin*

We all know the delicious smell of mown grass that comes off a meadow. The smell of 'Old Man' or 'Lad's-Love' – a bush of it grew in his garden – baffled the poet Edward Thomas. Crumbling a leaf, he felt he was on the very edge of remembering what its bitter fragrance reminded him of. But he never did quite recall the memory – it was buried too deep. And it was out of his failure to remember that he made this marvellous poem of his. You see, poems can be written from not knowing the answers. Perhaps they always are.

> Old Man, or Lad's-love,—in the name there's nothing
> To one that knows not Lad's-love, or Old Man,
> The hoar-green feathery herb, almost a tree,
> Growing with rosemary and lavender.
> Even to one that knows it well, the names
> Half decorate, half perplex, the thing it is:
> At least, what that is clings not to the names

In spite of time. And yet I like the names.
The herb itself I like not, but for certain
I love it, as some day the child will love it
Who plucks a feather from the door-side bush
Whenever she goes in or out of the house.
Often she waits there, snipping the tips and shrivelling
The shreds at last on to the path,
Thinking, perhaps of nothing, till she sniffs
Her fingers and runs off. The bush is still
But half as tall as she, though it is as old;
So well she clips it. Not a word she says;
And I can only wonder how much hereafter
She will remember, with that bitter scent,
Of garden rows, and ancient damson trees
Topping a hedge, a bent path to a door,
A low thick bush beside the door, and me
Forbidding her to pick.

                       As for myself,
Where first I met the bitter scent is lost.
I, too, often shrivel the grey shreds,
Sniff them and think and sniff again and try
Once more to think what it is I am remembering,
Always in vain. I cannot like the scent,
Yet I would rather give up others more sweet,
With no meaning, than this bitter one.
I have mislaid the key. I sniff the spray
And think of nothing; I see and I hear nothing;
Yet seem, too, to be listening, lying in wait
For what I should, yet never can, remember:
No garden appears, no path, no hoar-green bush
Of Lad's-love or Old Man, no child beside,
Neither father nor mother, nor any playmate;
Only an avenue, dark, nameless, without end.

'Old Man'
by Edward Thomas

DEATH
AND
IMMORTALITY

How fresh, O Lord, how sweet and clean
Are thy returns! even as the flowers in spring;
To which, besides their own demean,
The late-past frosts tributes of pleasure bring.
Grief melts away
Like snow in May,
As if there were no such cold thing.

Who would have thought my shrivell'd heart
Could have recover'd greenness? It was gone
Quite under ground; as flowers depart
To see their Mother-root, when they have blown;
Where they together
All the hard weather,
Dead to the world, keep house unknown.

These are thy wonders, Lord of power,
Killing and quickening, bringing down to hell
And up to heaven in an hour;
Making a chiming of a passing bell.
We say amiss,
This or that is:
Thy word is all, if we could spell.

O that I once past changing were,
Fast in thy Paradise, where no flower can wither!
Many a spring I shoot up fair,
Offering at heaven growing and groaning thither:

Nor doth my flower
Want a spring-shower,
My sins and I joining together.

But while I grow in a straight line,
Still upwards bent, as if heaven were mine own,
Thy anger comes, and I decline:
What frost to that? what pole is not the zone
Where all things burn,
When thou dost turn,
And the least frown of thine is shown?

And now in age I bud again,
After so many deaths I live and write;
I once more smell the dew and rain,
And relish versing: O my only light,
It cannot be
That I am he,
On whom thy tempests fell all night.

from 'The Flower'
by George Herbert

As a poet I am always greatly moved by those lines 'And now in age I bud again, After so many deaths I live and write . . . And relish versing'.

And now, another marvellous poem out of that great age of English religious poetry, the seventeenth century. This is a poem called 'The Exequy' which Bishop King wrote after the death of his wife.

Sleep on, my love, in thy cold bed,
Never to be disquieted!
My last good night! Thou wilt not wake,
Till I thy fate shall overtake;
Till age, or grief, or sickness, must

Marry my body to that dust
It so much loves; and fill the room
My heart keeps empty in thy tomb.
Stay for me there; I will not fail
To meet thee in that hollow vale:
And think not much of my delay;
I am already on the way,
And follow thee with all the speed
Desire can make, or sorrows breed.
Each minute is a short degree,
And ev'ry hour a step towards thee.
At night, when I betake to rest,
Next morn I rise nearer my West
Of life, almost by eight hours' sail,
Than when sleep breath'd his drowsy gale.

   Thus from the Sun my bottom steers,
And my day's compass downward bears;
Nor labour I to stem the tide,
Through which to *thee* I swiftly glide.

'Tis true, with shame and grief I yield,
Thou, like the van, first took'st the field,
And gotten hast the victory,
In thus adventuring to die
Before me, whose more years might crave
A just precedence in the grave.
But hark! My pulse, like a soft drum,
Beats my approach, tells *thee* I come;
And slow howe'er my marches be,
I shall at last sit down by *thee*.

   The thought of this bids me go on,
And wait my dissolution

With hope and comfort. Dear (forgive
The crime), I am content to live
Divided, with but half a heart,
Till we shall meet and never part.

from 'The Exequy'
by Henry King

❋

And to reinforce that idea of the happy acceptance of death, happy because men believed that death was a gateway into an eternal life, here is another seventeenth-century jewel, Henry Vaughan's poem, 'They're all gone into the world of light!'

They are all gone into the world of light!
   And I alone sit ling'ring here;
Their very memory is fair and bright,
     And my sad thoughts doth clear.

It glows and glitters in my cloudy breast,
   Like stars upon some gloomy grove,
Or those faint beams in which this hill is dress'd,
     After the sun's remove.

I see them walking in an air of glory,
   Whose light doth trample on my days:
My days, which are at best but dull and hoary,
     Mere glimmering and decays.

O holy Hope! and high Humility,
   High as the heavens above!
These are your walks, and you have show'd them me,
     To kindle my cold love.

Dear, beauteous Death! the jewel of the just,
   Shining nowhere, but in the dark;
What mysteries do lie beyond thy dust,
     Could man outlook that mark!

He that hath found some fledg'd bird's nest, may know
　　At first sight, if the bird be flown;
But what fair well or grove he sings in now,
　　That is to him unknown.

And yet, as angels in some brighter dreams
　　Call to the soul when man doth sleep,
So some strange thoughts transcend our wonted themes,
　　And into glory peep.

If a star were confin'd into a tomb,
　　Her captive flames must needs burn there;
But when the hand that lock'd her up, gives room,
　　She'll shine through all the sphere.

O Father of eternal life, and all
　　Created glories under Thee!
Resume Thy spirit from this world of thrall
　　Into true liberty.

Either disperse these mists, which blot and fill
　　My perspective still as they pass:
Or else remove me hence unto that hill
　　Where I shall need no glass.

Henry Vaughan

Something very different now, written centuries before those last three poems, but it may fit more precisely our modern ideas about the state of mind with which we reflect upon – attempt to reflect upon – the nature of God. You remember when God, after visiting a succession of very heavy and we may think very undeserved sufferings upon Job, comes out of the whirlwind to speak to him, God does not attempt to justify himself, he doesn't say I sent you these sufferings to try you, to test your Faith – not a bit of it. What he did say was to point out with superb eloquence – the finest, I think, in the Old

Testament – that no man can pit his human ideas of justice and injustice against the illimitable powers and the inscrutable nature of the Supreme Being, the Creator of all human beings and all animals – all the whole Creation.

Then the Lord answered Job out of the whirlwind, and said,
2 Who *is* this that darkeneth counsel by words without knowledge?
3 Gird up now thy loins like a man; for I will demand of thee, and answer thou me.
4 Where wast thou when I laid the foundations of the earth? declare, if thou hast understanding.
5 Who hath laid the measures thereof, if thou knowest? or who hath stretched the line upon it?
6 Whereupon are the foundations thereof fastened? or who laid the corner stone thereof;
7 When the morning stars sang together, and all the sons of God shouted for joy?
8 Or *who* shut up the sea with doors, when it brake forth, *as if* it had issued out of the womb?
9 When I made the cloud the garment thereof, and thick darkness a swaddlingband for it,
10 And brake up for it my decreed *place*, and set bars and doors,
11 And said, Hitherto shalt thou come, but no further: and here shall thy proud waves be stayed?
12 Hast thou commanded the morning since thy days; *and* caused the dayspring to know his place;
13 That it might take hold of the ends of the earth, that the wicked might be shaken out of it?
14 It is turned as clay *to* the seal; and they stand as a garment.
15 And from the wicked their light is withholden, and the high arm shall be broken.
16 Hast thou entered into the springs of the sea? or hast thou walked in the search of the depth?
17 Have the gates of death been opened unto thee? or hast thou seen the doors of the shadow of death?

18 Hast thou perceived the breadth of the earth? declare if thou knowest it all.

19 Where *is* the way *where* light dwelleth? and *as for* darkness, where *is* the place thereof,

20 That thou shouldest take it to the bound thereof, and that thou shouldest know the paths *to* the house thereof?

21 Knowest thou *it*, because thou wast then born? or *because* the number of thy days *is* great?

22 Hast thou entered into the treasures of the snow? or hast thou seen the treasures of the hail,

23 Which I have reserved against the time of trouble, against the day of battle and war?

24 By what way is the light parted, *which* scattereth the east wind upon the earth?

25 Who hath divided a watercourse for the overflowing of waters, or a way for the lightning of thunder;

26 To cause it to rain on the earth, *where* no man *is*; *on* the wilderness, wherein *there is* no man;

27 To satisfy the desolate and waste *ground*; and to cause the bud of the tender herb to spring forth?

28 Hath the rain a father? or who hath begotten the drops of dew?

29 Out of whose womb came the ice? and the hoary frost of heaven, who hath gendered it?

30 The waters are hid as *with* a stone, and the face of the deep is frozen.

31 Canst thou bind the sweet influences of Pleiades, or loose the bands of Orion?

32 Canst thou bring forth Mazzaroth in his season? or canst thou guide Arcturus with his sons?

33 Knowest thou the ordinances of heaven? canst thou set the dominion thereof in the earth?

34 Canst thou lift up thy voice to the clouds, that abundance of waters may cover thee?

35 Canst thou send lightnings, that they may go, and say unto thee, Here we *are*?

36 Who hath put wisdom in the inward parts? or who hath given understanding to the heart?
37 Who can number the clouds in wisdom? or who can stay the bottles of heaven,
38 When the dust groweth into hardness, and the clods cleave fast together?
39 Wilt thou hunt the prey for the lion? or fill the appetite of the young lions,
40 When they couch in *their* dens, *and* abide in the covert to lie in wait?
41 Who provideth for the raven his food? when his young ones cry unto God, they wander for lack of meat.

The Book of Job
Chapter 38

The nineteenth-century American poet, Emily Dickinson, was much possessed by death. She was an intense poet, an unorthodox religious poet, and she had the kind of originality which can, as it were, squeeze a commonplace situation and distil again from it its precious essence. I expect most of you know the cliché about 'every parting is a little death'. Here's what Emily Dickinson made of it.

My life closed twice before its close;
　　It yet remains to see
If Immortality unveil
　　A third event to me,

So huge, so hopeless to conceive,
　　As these that twice befell.
Parting is all we know of heaven,
　　And all we need of hell.

Emily Dickinson

You see, Emily Dickinson does keep an open mind about what she'll find behind the veil of immortality.

Now there s another way of looking at death and it's a way very largely confined to poets of our own century, the way of anguished, desperate protest, in which ideas of God hardly enter at all. The piece below is 'Futility'. It was written by Wilfred Owen, who himself was killed during the last few days of the First World War.

Move him into the sun—
Gently its touch awoke him once,
At home, whispering of fields unsown.
Always it woke him, even in France,
Until this morning and this snow.
If anything might rouse him now
The kind old sun will know.

Think how it wakes the seeds,—
Woke, once, the clays of a cold star.
Are limbs, so dear-achieved, are sides,
Full-nerved—still warm—too hard to stir?
Was it for this the clay grew tall?
—O what made fatuous sunbeams toil
To break earth's sleep at all?

'Futility'
by Wilfred Owen

�֍

The next poem is by Dylan Thomas. This poem is more than just a poem of protest against Man's inevitable end, it's a kind of squaring up to death. He had his own father's dying in mind when he wrote it. It's a great cry of courage and for courage in the face of Man's death. Let's fight to the bitter end, the poem says, although we know we're fighting a losing battle, and above all let us not peter out tamely.

Do not go gentle into that good night,
Old age should burn and rave at close of day;
Rage, rage against the dying of the light.

Though wise men at their end know dark is right,
Because their words have forked no lightning they
Do not go gentle into that good night.

Good men, the last wave by, crying how bright
Their frail deeds might have danced in a green bay,
Rage, rage against the dying of the light.

Wild men who caught and sang the sun in flight,
And learn, too late, they grieved it on its way,
Do not go gentle into that good night.

Grave men, near death, who see with blinding sight
Blind eyes could blaze like meteors and be gay,
Rage, rage against the dying of the light.

And you, my father, there on the sad height,
Curse, bless, me now with your fierce tears, I pray.
Do not go gentle into that good night.
Rage, rage against the dying of the light.

Dylan Thomas

*And here, by contrast, let me put in Yeats's 'An Irish Airman Fore-
sees his Death'. The contrast is in the tone. The Dylan Thomas poem
and the Wilfred Owen poem are violent and personal. Yeats's poem
strikes one as very impersonal, although, in fact, he knew the hero
of it, who was indeed killed in the air, fighting in the air, in the First
World War, because it was a son of Lady Gregory, Yeats's great
friend. But it's a call, as 'Do not go gentle' is, but this time almost a
happy one, to a last struggle. As Yeats puts it, 'A lonely impulse of
delight drove to this tumult in the clouds'.*

I know that I shall meet my fate
Somewhere among the clouds above;
Those that I fight I do not hate,
Those that I guard I do not love;
My country is Kiltartan Cross,

My countrymen Kiltartan's poor,
No likely end could bring them loss
Or leave them happier than before.
Nor law, nor duty bade me fight,
Nor public men, nor cheering crowds,
A lonely impulse of delight
Drove to this tumult in the clouds;
I balanced all, brought all to mind,
The years to come seemed waste of breath,
A waste of breath the years behind
In balance with this life, this death.

*'An Irish Airman Foresees his Death'
by W. B. Yeats*

*We end, as we should do, with Shakespeare. Shakespeare held out
no conventional religious hope of immortality. But in a few of his
sonnets he does convey a sort of humanist message; he says that a
man may live on after death through the eternal lines of poetry.*

Shall I compare thee to a Summer's day?
Thou art more lovely and more temperate:
Rough winds do shake the darling buds of May,
And Summer's lease hath all too short a date:
Sometime too hot the eye of heaven shines,
And often is his gold complexion dimm'd;
And every fair from fair sometime declines,
By chance or nature's changing course, untrimm'd:
But thy eternal Summer shall not fade
Nor lose possession of that fair thou owest;
Nor shall Death brag thou wanderest in his shade,
When in eternal lines to time thou growest:
  So long as men can breathe, or eyes can see,
  So long lives this, and this gives life to thee.

William Shakespeare

And to close with a dying fall, the incomparably gentle, incomparably accepting tone of 'Fear no more the heat of the sun'.

Fear no more the heat o' the sun,
    Nor the furious winter's rages;
Thou thy wordly task hast done,
    Home art gone and ta'en thy wages:
Golden lads and girls all must,
As chimney-sweepers, come to dust.

Fear no more the frown o' the great;
    Thou art past the tyrant's stroke:
Care no more to clothe and eat;
    To thee the reed is as the oak:
The sceptre, learning, physic, must
All follow this and come to dust.

Fear no more the lightning-flash,
    Nor the all-dreaded thunder-stone;
Fear not slander, censure rash;
    Thou hast finish'd joy and moan:
All lovers young, all lovers must
Consign to thee, and come to dust.

No exorciser harm thee!
Nor no witchcraft charm thee!
Ghost unlaid forbear thee!
Nothing ill come near thee!
Quiet consummation have;
And renowned be thy grave!

William Shakespeare

106

ACKNOWLEDGEMENTS

Grateful acknowledgement is due for the poems and extracts listed below to:

Curtis Brown, Macmillan London and Basingstoke, and the Macmillan Company of Canada for permission to include 'The Self-Unseeing' and 'At Castle Boterel' by Thomas Hardy; David Higham Associates and Dent & Sons Ltd for 'Do not go gentle into that good night' by Dylan Thomas; Feffer & Simons, Inc. for the extract from 'Gilgamesh' translated by Herbert Mason; George Allen & Unwin Ltd for Arthur Waley's translations of the three poems by Po Chü-i; Hogarth Press Ltd and Harcourt Brace Jovanovich, Inc. for 'A Sovereign from Western Libya' and 'Afternoon Sun' by C. P. Cavafy, translated by Rae Dalven and John Mavrogordato respectively; Ikaros and The Bodley Head for 'Mythistorema' and The 'Thrush' by George Seferis, and Rex Warner for his translation of these two poems; Jonathan Cape Ltd and the Hogarth Press for 'In the Shelter', and Jonathan Cape Ltd for the extracts from 'For Rex Warner on his Sixtieth Birthday' and the translation of Virgil's Fourth Eclogue, all by C. Day Lewis; Laurence Pollinger Ltd and Heinemann Ltd for 'Humming-Bird' by D. H. Lawrence; Philip Larkin for 'Cut Grass'; and the Society of Authors, A. P. Watt & Son, Macmillan London and Basingstoke, and Macmillan Canada for 'In Memory of Eva Gore-Booth and Con Markiewicz' and 'An Irish Airman Foresees his Death' by W. B. Yeats.

These poems and extracts can be found in the following books:

Part I
'Humming-Bird' by D. H. Lawrence, from the *Complete Poems of D. H. Lawrence,* with Introduction and Notes by Vivian de Sola Pinto and Warren Roberts (Heinemann, 1972).
'The Self-Unseeing' by Thomas Hardy, from *Selected Shorter Poems by Thomas Hardy,* edited by John Wain (Macmillan, 1966).

Extract from Fourth Eclogue in *The Eclogues of Virgil*, translated by C. Day Lewis (Cape, 1963).

'Golden Bells' and 'Remembering Golden Bells' by Po Chü-i, from *One Hundred and Seventy Chinese Poems*, translated by Arthur Waley (Constable, 1962).

Part II

'In the Shelter' by C. Day Lewis, from *The Collected Poems of C. Day Lewis* (Cape, 1954).

'Mythistorema' Part IV of 'Argonauts' by George Seferis, from *The Poems of George Seferis*, translated by Rex Warner (Bodley Head, 1960).

'Gilgamesh: A Verse Narrative' translated by Herbert Mason (Boston, Houghton, Mifflin & Co., 1971).

'In Memory of Eva Gore-Booth and Con Markiewicz' by W. B Yeats, from *The Collected Poems of W. B. Yeats* (Macmillan, 1961).

Part III

'A Sovereign from Western Libya' by C. P. Cavafy, from the *Complete Poems of C. P. Cavafy*, translated by Rae Dalven (Hogarth Press, 1961).

Part IV

'Dreaming that I Went with Li and Yü to visit Yüan Chên' by Po Chü-i, translated by Arthur Waley, from *Madly Singing in the Mountains: Appreciation and Anthology of Arthur Waley*, edited by Ivan Morris (Allen & Unwin, 1970).

The 'Thrush' by George Seferis, from *The Poems of George Seferis*, translated by Rex Warner (Bodley Head, 1960).

'For Rex Warner on his Sixtieth Birthday' by C. Day Lewis, from *The Room and Other Poems* by C. Day Lewis (Cape, 1965).

'At Castle Boterel' by Thomas Hardy, from the *Collected Poems of Thomas Hardy* (Macmillan, 1930).

'Afternoon Sun' by C. P. Cavafy, from the *Complete Poems of C. P. Cavafy*, translated by John Mavrogordato (Hogarth Press, 1971).

Part V

'Cut Grass' by Philip Larkin (not yet published).

Part VI

'Do not go gentle into that good night' by Dylan Thomas, from *Collected Poems of Dylan Thomas* (Dent, 1952).

'An Irish Airman Foresees his Death' by W. B. Yeats, from *Faber Book of Modern Verse*, edited by Michael Roberts (Faber, 1965).

INDEX

Blake, William
'Milton' 83
Brontë, Emily
'R. Alcona to J. Brenzaida'
(Remembrance) 64
Browning, Robert
'My Last Duchess' 48
'Two in the Campagna' 65
Byron, Lord
'The Vision of Judgement' 53

Carew, Thomas
Ask me no more where Jove bestows
72
Cavafy, C. P.
'The Afternoon Sun' 74
'A Sovereign from Western
Libya' 60
Clough, Arthur Hugh
'Amours de Voyage' 58
Coleridge, Samuel Taylor
'Dejection: an Ode' 79
Collins, William
'Ode to Evening' 88
Cowper, William
'On Receipt of my Mother's
Picture out of Norfolk' 28
Crabbe, George
'The Parish Register' 56

Dibdin, Charles
'Tom Bowling' 70
Dickinson, Emily
My life closed twice before its close
102

Dobell, Sidney
'The Orphan's Song' 24
Dryden, John
'Absalom and Achitophel' 37

Gay, John
'Trivia' 85
Goldsmith, Oliver
'The Deserted Village' 38

Hardy, Thomas
'At Castle Boterel' 75
'The Self-Unseeing' 29
Herbert, George
'The Flower' 95
Hood, Thomas
'Past and Present' 17
Hopkins, Gerard Manley
'Spring and Fall' 22

Job, The Book of, Chapter 38 100

King, Henry
'The Exequy' 96

Larkin, Philip
'Cut Grass' 90
Lawrence, D. H.
'Humming-Bird' 27
Lewis, C. Day
'For Rex Warner on His Sixtieth
Birthday' 70
'In the Shelter' 35

Mason, Herbert (trs.)
'Gilgamesh' 41

Owen, Wilfred
'Futility' 103

Po Chü-i
'Dreaming that I Went with Li
and Yü to Visit Yüan Chên' 71
'Golden Bells' 23
'Remembering Golden Bells' 23
Pope, Alexander
'Epistle to Dr Arbuthnot' 52
'An Essay on Man' 33
Praed, W. M.
'A Letter of Advice' 68

Seferis, George
'Mythistorema' 39
The 'Thrush' 73
Shakespeare, William
Fear no more the heat o' the sun 106
Shall I compare thee to a Summer's
day? 105

Tennyson, Alfred Lord
'The New Timon and the Poets'
50
'Ulysses' 44
Thomas, Dylan
Do not go gentle into that good
night 103
Thomas, Edward
'Old Man' 90

Thomson, James
'The City of Dreadful Night' 86
Thomson, James
'Winter' 83
traditional ballad
'The Brown Girl' 47
Traherne, Thomas
'The Salutation' 18

Vaughan, Henry
They are all gone into the world of
light! 98
Virgil
'Fourth Eclogue' 26

Whitman, Walt
'There Was a Child Went Forth'
19
Wolfe, Charles
'The Burial of Sir John Moore
after Corunna' 34
Wordsworth, William
'Intimations of Immortality from
Recollections of Early Child-
hood' 19
'Lines Composed a Few Miles
above Tintern Abbey' 81
Wyatt, Sir Thomas
'They Flee from Me' 63

Yeats, W. B.
'In Memory of Eva Gore-Booth
and Con Markiewicz' 43
'An Irish Airman Foresees his
Death' 104